SCIENCE FOR LIFE AND LIVING
INTEGRATING SCIENCE, TECHNOLOGY, AND HEALTH

Systems and Analysis

BSCS *Innovative Science Education*

founded 1958

KENDALL/HUNT PUBLISHING COMPANY
2460 Kerper Boulevard P.O. Box 539 Dubuque, Iowa 52004-0539

Acknowledgments begin on page 313.

ISBN 0–8403–5996–9

This material is based on work supported by the National Science Foundation under grant No. MDR-8652131, the Adolph Coors Foundation of Colorado, the Gates Foundation of Colorado, and IBM Educational Systems of Atlanta, Georgia. Any opinions, findings, and conclusions or recommendations expressed in this publication are those of the author(s) and do not necessarily reflect the views of the granting agencies.

10 9 8 7 6 5 4 3 2 1

Contributors

Mary Sue Baker, Boulder, Colorado, free-lance writer, Level 3

Nancy Booth, Madison, Wisconsin, free-lance writer, Level K

Katherine Corley, Towson, Maryland, free-lance writer, Level 4

Cathy Griswold, Lyons, Oregon, free-lance writer, Levels K and 1

Debra Hannigan, Colorado Springs, Colorado, free-lance writer, Level 6

Michael Hannigan, Colorado Springs, Colorado, field coordinator

Mark Hartwig, Colorado Springs, Colorado, evaluation

Evelyn Lee, Fairchild, Connectiuct, free-lance writer, Level 2

Janet Carlson Powell, Colorado Springs, Colorado, free-lance writer, Level 3

Nellie Rost, Flagstaff, Arizona, Enrichment Through Children's Literature

Laurel Sherman, Oberlin, Ohio, free-lance writer, Level 4

Maria Weisenberg, St. James, New York, free-lance writer, Level 6

Consultants

Thomas Anderson, Center for the Study of Reading, University of Illinois, Champaign, Illinois, reading in the content areas

Gregory Borsinger, American Cyanamid Company, Wayne, New Jersey ("Strange Stuff," Level 2)

Judy Braus, National Wildlife Federation, Washington, D.C., reading in the content areas

Catherine Burnham, Center for the Study of Reading, University of Illinois, Champaign, Illinois, reading in the content areas

Audrey Champagne, State University of New York at Albany, Albany, New York, cognitive development

Del DeMuth, Lewis Palmer Elementary School, Monument, Colorado (Awareness of Space, Level K)

Jack Gerlovich, Drake University, Des Moines, Iowa, safety in the science classroom

Gene Hall, University of Northern Colorado, Greeley, Colorado, implementation

Norris Harms, Arvada, Colorado, evaluation

Arlene Hirschfelder, Teaneck, New Jersey, Native American Studies ("Laughing Lark," Level 2)

Roger Johnson, Cooperative Learning Center, University of Minnesota, Minneapolis, Minnesota, cooperative learning

Tamara Keller, Denver, Colorado, reading in the content areas

Betty Kistler, Water Mill, New York, technology

Joseph Novak, Cornell University, Ithaca, New York, cognitive development

E. Joseph Piel, professor emeritus, State University of New York at Stony Brook, Stony Brook, New York, technology

William Rutherford, University of Texas at Austin, Austin, Texas, implementation

Daniel J. Wofford, Jr., Western Polyacrylamide, Inc., Castle Rock, Colorado ("Strange Stuff," Level 2)

Reviewers

Thomas Anderson, Champaign, Illinois, reading and science education

Catherine Balsley, Philadelphia, Pennsylvania, substance abuse prevention and urban health education

James Barufaldi, Austin, Texas, science education

Roberta Beach, Denver, Colorado, adolescent health

Carl Berger, Ann Arbor, Michigan, science education

Nancy Booth, Madison, Wisconsin, primary education

Heather Brasell, Alapaha, Georgia, cooperative learning

Judy Braus, Washington, D.C., reading and science education

Catherine Burnham, Champaign, Illinois, reading

Audrey Champagne, Albany, New York, physical science

Eileen Earhart, Tallahassee, Florida, early childhood education

James Ebersole, Colorado Springs, Colorado, ecology

Donnie Espinoza, Colorado Springs, Colorado, physical education

April Gardner, Greeley, Colorado, equity issues

Yolanda George, Washington, D.C., equity issues

Jack Gerlovich, Des Moines, Iowa, safety in the science classroom

Cathy Griswold, Lyons, Oregon, primary education

Mario Iona, Denver, Colorado, physical science

Brent Jackson, Boston, Massachusetts, technology

Tamara Keller, Denver, Colorado, reading

Gregory Kroll, Yellowstone National Park, Wyoming, ecology

David LaHart, Cape Canaveral, Florida, science education

Patricia Legos, Philadelphia, Pennsylvania, nutrition education

Thomas Liao, Stony Brook, New York, technology

Lisa Lieberman, New York, New York, health education

Marcia Linn, Berkeley, California, technology and science education

Walter MacDonald, Princeton, New Jersey, assessment

Fidelia Maez, Denver, Colorado, adolescent health

Alan McCormack, San Diego, California, science education

Marge Melle, Littleton, Colorado, primary education and cooperative learning

Cheryl Norton, Golden, Colorado, exercise physiology

Martha Owens, Ocilla, Georgia, early childhood education

Rod Peturson, Windsor, Ontario, science education

E. Joseph Piel, Stony Brook, New York, technology

William Rutherford, Austin, Texas, implementation

Debra Sandau-Christopher, Denver, Colorado, sexual abuse prevention and HIV education

Alan Sandler, Washington, D.C., technology and design

David Sleet, La Jolla, California, injury prevention

Patricia Smith, Colorado Springs, Colorado, science education

Joseph Stepans, Laramie, Wyoming, science education

Joan Tephley, Davenport, Iowa, early childhood education

Jerrold Thompson, Lakewood, Colorado, dental health

IMPORTANT: Please be advised that use of *Science for Life and Living* requires goggles. Students will use a variety of common objects and materials (for example, rubber bands, hammers, and screwdrivers, and household chemicals such as vinegar) whose use requires eye protection. Standardized safety goggles are required to be used with *Science for Life and Living* as indicated in the program, without exception.

CONTENTS

UNIT
1

Introduction to the Year's Themes
SYSTEMS AND ANALYSIS

Introduction

Hello and welcome to _Science for Life and Living_! I think you'll like science this year. It's fun because you can do interesting experiments, and you can work with a teammate. My teammate is C.Q. He likes science, too.

Hi! I'm C.Q. K.T. and I make a good team. She helps me figure things out, and I help her try different ideas. Working together helps us learn more because two heads are better than one!

This year, you'll work with teammates who can help you learn, too. Sometimes, you'll work with your friends. Other times, you'll work with teammates you don't know as well. With so many different teammates, you should learn a lot!

Team Skills

C.Q. and K.T. know that it takes skill to work with others. A good team doesn't just happen. You have to work at it. You can learn many skills to help you work successfully in teams. Here are five team skills you should practice every time you work as a team.

1. **Move into your teams quickly and quietly.**

2. **Speak softly.**

3. **Stay with your teams.**

4. **Take turns.**

5. **Do your jobs.**

The first three skills are pretty easy to practice. When your teacher tells you to meet with your team, find your teammates right away. Go directly to your team's meeting place without stopping to talk along the way. When you talk with your teammates, keep your voice down so you don't bother nearby teams. Staying with your team is also easy to do if you try.

The skill of taking turns can be harder to practice. You and your teammates must make sure that everyone on the team gets to do part of each task. One way to make sure is to ask one another, "Have you had a chance to try this yet?" Whoever says no gets to go next.

To practice the fifth skill, you need to know four different jobs. Your teacher will assign one of these jobs to you each time your team meets. You won't always practice the same job, and some jobs might seem easier than others. Read the following job descriptions to help you understand how to do each job.

Team Jobs

The **communicator** may ask the teacher or another team's communicator for help if the team gets stuck. For instance, if your team can't read a direction, the communicator could ask the teacher for help. Or, if the teacher is busy, the communicator could ask another team's communicator for help. Only the communicator should ask for help, though. Everyone else should stay with the team.

The **manager** picks up and returns the team's supplies. Look for a section on the page that looks like this:

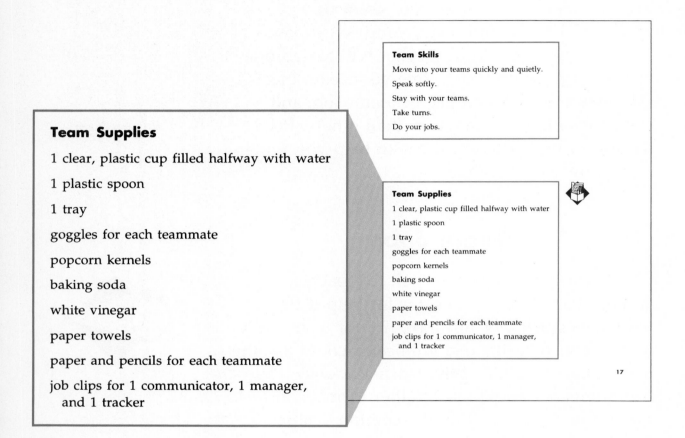

Team Supplies

1 clear, plastic cup filled halfway with water

1 plastic spoon

1 tray

goggles for each teammate

popcorn kernels

baking soda

white vinegar

paper towels

paper and pencils for each teammate

job clips for 1 communicator, 1 manager, and 1 tracker

Team Skills

Move into your teams quickly and quietly.

Speak softly.

Stay with your teams.

Take turns.

Do your jobs.

Team Supplies

1 clear, plastic cup filled halfway with water

1 plastic spoon

1 tray

goggles for each teammate

popcorn kernels

baking soda

white vinegar

paper towels

paper and pencils for each teammate

job clips for 1 communicator, 1 manager, and 1 tracker

17

The manager gets the supplies listed under Team Supplies. When the team finishes the team task, everyone should help clean up the work area. Then, the manager returns the supplies.

The **tracker** keeps track of which step of the directions the team is doing. Look for steps that look like this:

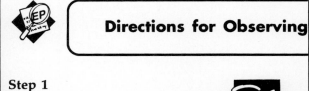

Directions for Observing

Step 1

Put on your goggles.

Directions for Observing the Dance

Step 1

Put on your goggles.

Yes!

No!

Step 2

Stir the baking soda into the cup of water.

To prevent messes, keep all the supplies on the tray.

18

The tracker makes sure that the team does every step. The tracker might point to each step as the team works on it. If the team needs to stop, the tracker might write down the number of the step the team needs to begin with later. Everyone on the team needs to help read and follow the directions. The tracker is not the team's reader.

The **checker** makes sure that the team knows what the team task is. The checker also reminds the team to complete the team task. Look for a section on the page that looks like this:

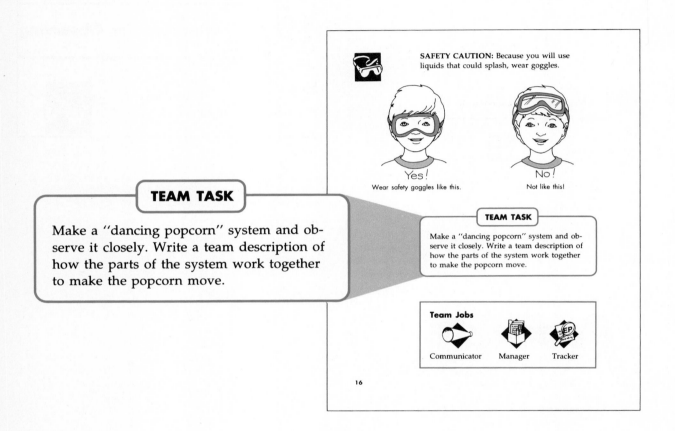

The checker makes sure that the team knows what the task is. The checker is not the boss. The whole team needs to decide how to complete the task so that everyone takes part. Later, when teammates think they have finished, the checker checks the team task again. If the teammates agree that they have completed the task, they may stop working.

Getting Started

The best way to learn how to use the team skills is to try them. You and your teammates will practice the team skills starting in the second lesson of this unit. Using the skills might feel strange at first, but you will get better each time you practice. Have fun learning science and learning to work together with your teammates.

A Fair Race?

K.T. and C.Q. are going to race down the slides. How can they be sure they are in a fair race?

Last one down is a rotten egg!

Racing Marbles

Now that you have talked about what makes a race fair, you can help your teacher conduct a fair race between a glass marble and a steel marble. Your job is to predict which marble will win the race.

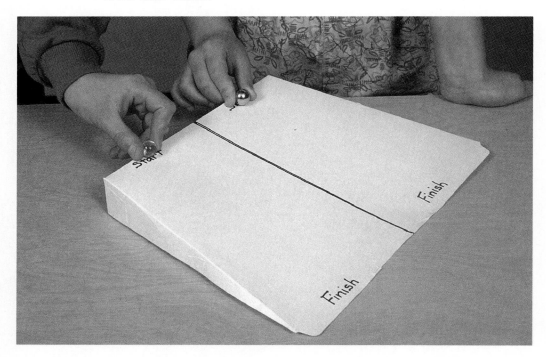

Wrap-up

With your classmates, discuss answers to these questions.

1. Was the race between the two marbles a fair race? Why or why not?

2. Why is it important to know all the parts of a system before you make a prediction?

LESSON 2

The Popcorn Polka

Have you ever seen popcorn dance the polka? In this lesson, the popcorn won't really dance, but the kernels will move around a lot.

Observing the Dance

You and your teammates will build a system that makes popcorn kernels move. Observe the popcorn kernels closely as they move. See if you can observe what is happening that makes the kernels appear to dance.

SAFETY CAUTION: Because you will use liquids that could splash, wear goggles.

Yes!

Wear safety goggles like this.

No!

Not like this!

TEAM TASK

Make a "dancing popcorn" system and observe it closely. Write a team description of how the parts of the system work together to make the popcorn move.

Team Jobs

Communicator

Manager

Tracker

Team Skills

Move into your teams quickly and quietly.

Speak softly.

Stay with your teams.

Take turns.

Do your jobs.

Team Supplies

1 clear, plastic cup filled halfway with water

1 plastic spoon

1 tray

goggles for each teammate

popcorn kernels

baking soda

white vinegar

paper towels

paper and pencils for each teammate

job clips for 1 communicator, 1 manager, and 1 tracker

Directions for Observing the Dance

Step 1

Put on your goggles.

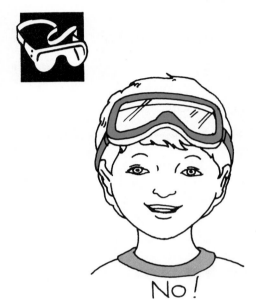

Yes!

No!

Step 2

Stir the baking soda into the cup of water.

To prevent messes, keep all the supplies on the tray.

Step 3

Put the popcorn kernels into the cup.

Remember to take turns. Make sure every teammate gets to do part of the task.

Step 4

Slowly pour the vinegar into the water and observe what happens.

Use the paper towels to wipe up any spills.

Step 5

Watch what happens until the popcorn kernels stop moving or until your teacher says to stop.

What happens to the popcorn kernels to make them move up? What happens to the popcorn kernels to make them move down again? What happens at the bottom of the glass? Does anything different happen at the top of the cup?

Step 6

On one sheet of paper, describe what teammates saw happen.

Write down everything teammates observed. Also describe what the team thinks made the popcorn move up and down.

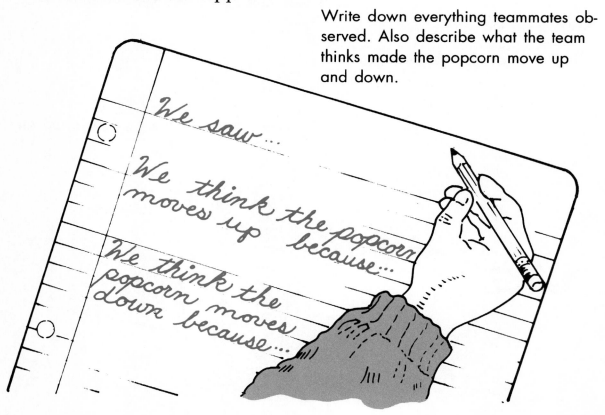

We saw...

We think the popcorn moves up because...

We think the popcorn moves down because...

Step 7

Use the team's observations to answer the Wrap-up questions.

You do not need goggles when you are talking and writing.

Discuss these questions with your teammates and agree on answers. Each teammate should write the answers on a sheet of paper.

1. What are the parts of the "dancing popcorn" system?

2. How do these parts work together to make the popcorn move?

3. How can the team get better at using the team skills?

What Is a System?

Look at the two drawings of the solar system. They were made at different times. What is the difference between the two drawings? Why do you think the two drawings are different? Read "The Mystery of Planet X" and find out.

Drawing of the Solar System, **1910**

Drawing of the Solar System, **1991**

*Planets are not really in a line nor equally spaced.
The book is not big enough to show distances.*

The Mystery of **Planet X**

Every night, astronomer Percival Lowell looked through the large telescope in his observatory. He loved to take pictures of the stars, planets, moon, comets, asteroids, and other objects in space. On one particular night, he sat in his observatory with pictures of the night sky spread all around him. Mr. Lowell was very puzzled. He leaned his chin on his hands and thought, "I know it's out there somewhere. It just has to be. Otherwise, why would Uranus and Neptune be out of orbit? I'm going to find Planet X if it kills me!"

Mr. Lowell was a very determined astronomer. He was trying to solve a very important mystery in the solar system—the mystery of Planet X.

Soon after astronomers discovered Neptune in 1846, they began to see that Uranus and Neptune were not moving around the sun exactly as they had predicted. Something seemed to be pulling Neptune and Uranus from their predicted orbits. What could it be? Astronomers called this mystery object Planet X, the unknown planet.

Mr. Lowell, who built the Lowell Observatory in Arizona, began to search the night sky. He used pictures of stars taken by his powerful telescopes at the observatory. He compared all his pictures, one with another, looking for something that moved differently than a star moved. He pored over his pictures, using a magnifying glass to study the tiny dots. He did this almost every day for eleven long years, but he was always disappointed. Time and again, he would find something that looked like it might be Planet X, but it would turn out to be an asteroid.

Some people think the search for Planet X did kill Mr. Lowell. The longer he kept searching, the more worn out he became. He lost weight and energy. He died of a stroke in 1916 without ever discovering the mysterious Planet X.

Even before the astronomer Lowell died, other astronomers became interested in the search. They could not find Planet X either. Then, a young astronomer by the name of Clyde W. Tombaugh tried to solve the mystery. In 1929, at the age of 23, Mr. Tombaugh began his search for Planet X. Later, he became an astronomer at the Lowell Observatory, taking up where Mr. Lowell left off thirteen years earlier.

By now, though, some equipment that made Mr. Tombaugh's search a little easier than Mr. Lowell's had been invented. The new equipment made it possible for Mr. Tombaugh to compare pictures of the stars by machine rather than by hand. The search was still not easy. Astronomer Tombaugh was looking for a very tiny object that was very far away in a sky filled with millions and millions of stars. It was like looking for a needle in a haystack. Some astronomers thought the task was impossible, but Clyde Tombaugh did not give up. He kept looking and looking.

The first pictures of Planet X

On February 18, 1930, Mr. Tombaugh spotted something different between two of his pictures. He found that a very small object had changed its position. He compared those two pictures with other pictures he had taken. Using all his pictures, Tombaugh traced a planet-like path for a short distance. When he showed his findings to other astronomers, they agreed with him. He had found Planet X!

An eleven-year-old English girl named Venetia Burney suggested the name for the ninth planet. She chose the name Pluto for the Roman god who ruled over the dark, cold underworld. Mr. Tombaugh and the staff of the Lowell Observatory liked the name. The new planet was far from the sun and would indeed be a cold and dark world. So, in 1930, mystery Planet X became Pluto, the ninth planet in the solar system.

Sun Mercury Venus Earth Mars Jupiter   Saturn   Neptune Uranus Pluto

Is this the end of the mystery? Is Pluto the last planet in the solar system? Some astronomers believe there must be a tenth planet beyond Pluto—another Planet X. They think this because Pluto is too small to have changed the orbits of Uranus and Neptune. Those astronomers are still searching for another Planet X, but not just with powerful telescopes. They hope that the Pioneer and

Voyager space probes might find evidence of another planet as the probes move beyond Uranus and Neptune. Astronomers think that satellites placed into orbit beyond the earth's atmosphere might beam back photographs of a tenth planet. No one is entirely sure, however, whether there is a new mystery Planet X.

Learning About Systems

A system is a group of objects that interact.

Dividing the world into systems, such as the solar system, helps people learn about how the world—and the universe—works. People learn about a system by studying how the parts of a system work together, or interact. Studying systems also helps people solve problems and make predictions.

For example, astronomers used their knowledge about how the solar system worked to discover the ninth planet, Pluto. The astronomers had already learned a lot about the movement of the first six planets around the sun. From that information, they were able to predict what the movement of Uranus and Neptune should have been. When the movement of Uranus and Neptune did not turn out to be what they expected, the astronomers looked for some reason to explain why those planets moved differently. Then, they found Pluto.

Remember the race between the glass and steel marbles in Lesson 1? Before your teacher switched the tracks of the marbles, you could make predictions about which marble would win. After your teacher switched the tracks, however, the steel marble rolled differently. You knew that something else was part of the system—something you had not seen before. You knew there must have been a magnet underneath the ramp because of the way the steel marble behaved.

When the planets Uranus and Neptune did not act as predicted, the astronomers knew they had to look further within the solar system. That is how astronomers solved the mystery of Planet X. You also had to look further within the ramp-and-marble system to understand why it worked as it did.

More About Interaction

Look again at the definition of a system on page 28. Do you know what the word "interact" means? If you do not, try this simple experiment.

Put a rubber band around your thumbs as shown, and carefully stretch it a short distance. (Be very careful that you do not stretch the rubber band so tightly that it either shoots off your thumbs or breaks.)

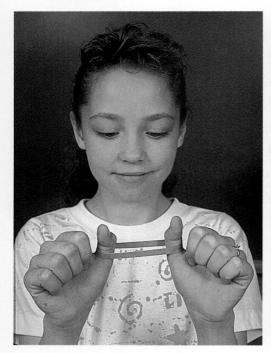

Objects interact when one object does something to another object or when both objects do something to each other. What objects interact during the rubber-band experiment? What is your evidence that the objects interact?

Usually, you can find evidence of interaction when one or both objects change in some way. By looking for change, you can often find evidence of an interaction.

Name some other objects that interact in some way. Think about objects you use in your classroom, at home, or on the playground. You can use your understanding of interactions to help you learn about systems.

Using a System to Solve a Problem

How can you use the idea of a system to help you solve a problem? Suppose you had a problem steering your bicycle. To solve your problem, it would help if you decided which parts of your bicycle were interacting to help you steer safely.

Which of the objects pictured below might be part of your bicycle's steering system? List the objects on a piece of paper.

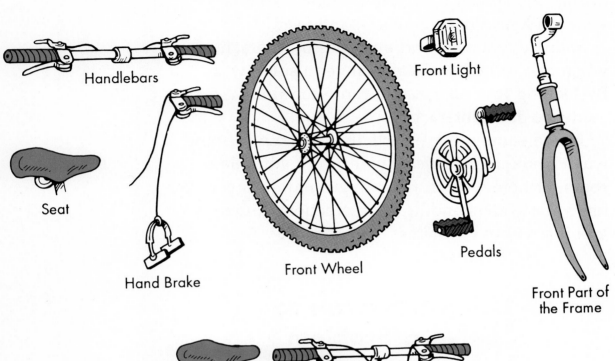

Handlebars

Seat

Hand Brake

Front Wheel

Front Light

Pedals

Front Part of the Frame

To fix your steering problem, you do not need to know about every part of your bike. You first have to decide which parts work together, or interact, to help you steer. When you decide which parts work together to steer your bike, you have chosen a system—your bicycle's steering system. Then, you need to compare the steering system of your bicycle with that of a bicycle that is working properly. If you look closely at how the parts of both steering systems are interacting, you might figure out why your bicycle does not steer very well. When you study both systems, you can compare what **is** happening to what **should be** happening. Then, you can fix the problem.

Deciding on a System

People divide objects in the world into systems so they can better explain what happens around them. For example, when early astronomers first looked into the sky, they saw many objects—clouds, the moon, planets, the sun, and thousands of stars. Because there were too many objects in the sky to study all at once, astronomers grouped objects that were related to one another into systems. They grouped some stars into constellations, such as the Big Dipper, Orion the hunter, and Draco the dragon. Later, astronomers realized that the planets revolved around the sun. They grouped the planets, the moons of the planets, and the sun into a system called the solar system.

Systems do not happen naturally in the world. People invented the idea of systems so they could study a few objects at a time. By dividing the world into systems, people could study just the parts they needed to help them understand how something worked.

People decide which objects to include in a system they want to study. Often, people decide what is part of the system by looking for ways objects interact.

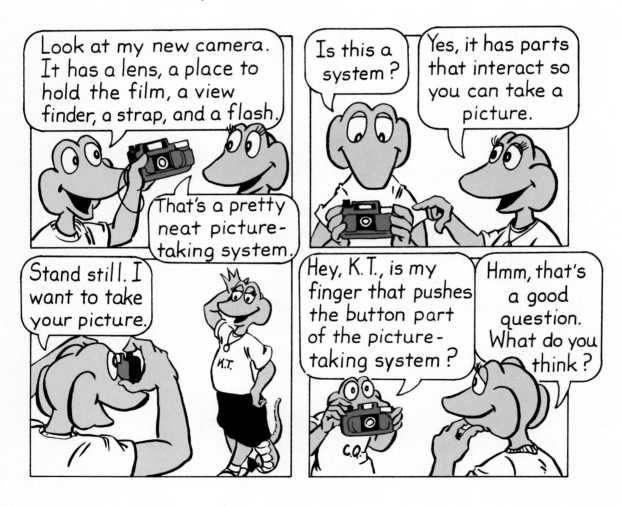

Do you think C.Q.'s finger should be part of his picture-taking system? Why or why not?

Actually, either way you decide is okay. People decide what goes into their system. Interactions help them decide what should be part of the system. People do not always choose the same parts when they study a system. Each person may decide to include different parts, depending on what he or she wants to find out. People choose parts that help them understand how the system works. What is important when you decide on a system is that you include everything that will help you describe what is happening.

Wrap-up

This lesson presented a lot of information about systems. Do not worry if you cannot remember all of it right now. You will have many chances to use this information as you work with systems in science class this year. Use information from this lesson to write answers to these questions.

1. What is a system? (Explain the word "system" using your own words.)

2. Give one example of a system at school or at home.

3. When someone hits a baseball with a bat, is there an interaction? What is your evidence?

Bottle Divers

Are you ready to find out about a new system? Your team will make a "bottle diver" and try to understand how it works.

Making the Diver

Before you can understand how a bottle diver works, you have to make one.

TEAM TASK

Make one bottle-diver system for the team.

Team Skills

Move into your teams quickly and quietly.

Speak softly.

Stay with your teams.

Take turns.

Do your jobs.

Team Jobs

Communicator   Manager   Tracker

Team Supplies

1 2-liter plastic bottle, full of water, with cap

1 dropper

1 pitcher, 3/4 full of water (you might have to share this with other teams)

job clips for 1 communicator, 1 manager, and 1 tracker

Directions for Making the Diver

Step 1

Using the water in the pitcher, fill the dropper about three-fourths full of water.

Remember to wipe up spills.

Step 2

Place the dropper into the water in the pitcher. See if it floats.

If it floats, go to Step 3. If it lies on its side, put more water in the dropper, and do Step 2 again. If it sinks, squeeze some water out of the dropper. Then, do Step 2 again.

Step 3

Place the dropper in the 2-liter plastic bottle.

It should float with the glass side down.

Step 4

Put the cap on the bottle tightly.

You have now made a bottle-diver system.

Step 5

Squeeze the sides of the bottle. Observe what happens to the dropper.

CAUTION

SAFETY CAUTION: Do not squeeze the bottle unless the cap is on all the way. Use both hands and squeeze hard. Why do you think this is called a "bottle-diver system"? Let everyone on your team have a chance to squeeze the bottle.

Step 6

Talk about whether the bottle diver is a system and why or why not.

Does it have parts? If so, what are the parts? Do the parts interact?

Introducing Analysis

When you separate a system into its parts to understand it, you are **analyzing** the system. People usually do not physically take the system apart to **analyze** it. They take the system apart in their imagination. When you named the parts of the bottle-diver system, you took it apart in your imagination. You started to **analyze** the system.

One way to **analyze** a system is to

• observe the system and see what happens,

• ask questions you can answer by observing,

• describe the evidence that things are interacting,

• identify the parts of the system, and

• answer your questions, to the best of your ability.

Some examples of analysis include the following:

• Chemists wanted to know what water was made of. They analyzed water and found that it was made of oxygen and hydrogen.

• Citizens wanted to understand how the parts of their government fit together, so they analyzed the way their government worked. The citizens identified the people (parts) who made the decisions that affected the citizens.

- Geologists wanted to know what minerals were in a rock. They analyzed the rock and found that one part of the rock was the mineral iron.

The things that are interacting are the **parts of the system.**

With your class, analyze the marble-racing system from Lesson 1, "A Fair Race?" Describe what you observed. Ask a question such as "Why did the steel marble stop on one side of the ramp?" Describe the evidence you found that things were interacting. Identify the parts of the system. Answer your question. If you had known all the parts of the system at the beginning, would you have made the same prediction?

An analysis of the marble-racing system might look like this:

Analysis of a Marble-Racing System

I **observed** that two marbles rolled down the ramp. When the steel ball was on one side of the ramp, it rolled straight down. When it was on the other side of the ramp, it stopped. The glass marble rolled straight down both sides of the ramp.

Why did the steel marble stop on one side of the ramp but not on the other?

Evidence of an interaction was that the steel marble stopped in the middle of one of the tracks.

The **parts of the system**: a steel marble, a glass marble, a ramp, and a hidden magnet.

The steel marble stopped **because** a magnet was hidden under one side of the ramp.

Analyze the Bottle-diver System

Do you have questions about the bottle-diver system? Could you answer those questions by observing the system closely? With your teammates, analyze the bottle-diver system.

TEAM TASK

Analyze the bottle-diver system. Be ready to explain your team's analysis and give your team's answers to the Wrap-up questions.

Team Skills

Move into your teams quickly and quietly.

Speak softly.

Stay with your teams.

Take turns.

Do your jobs.

Team Jobs

 Communicator Tracker Checker

Team Supplies

the team's bottle-diver system

pencil and paper

job clips for 1 communicator, 1 tracker, and
1 checker

Directions for Analyzing
the Bottle-diver System

Step 1

Observe what happens in the
bottle-diver system.

Squeeze the bottle, make the dropper dive, and continue to observe
the system.

Step 2

On a sheet of paper, write some questions your team has about the bottle-diver system.

Step 3

Describe the evidence that parts of the system interacted.

Step 4

List the parts of the system.

Did you include every part you said interacted in Step 3?

Step 5

Use your observations and answer the questions you asked in Step 2.

In your answer, use the parts and the interactions you identified.

Step 6

Talk about this question: How did analyzing help you answer a question about the bottle-diver system?

Did identifying the interactions between parts help you? Did you find any new parts you did not observe at first?

Step 7

As a team, answer the Wrap-up questions.

CHECKER: Can everyone explain the team's analysis? Has the team done a complete analysis? Has the team finished the team task?

Together with your team, discuss these questions.

1. In what ways is analyzing a system useful?

2. What are the parts of your team's system?

3. How could you improve the interactions between the parts of your team's system?

The Case of the Sick Friends

Sniff . . . Cough . . . Sneeze . . . A cold is a very common disease. Do you remember how you felt the last time you had a cold? You probably felt bad and hoped to get well quickly. Wouldn't it be nice not to catch colds? If you knew how you got a cold, maybe you could find ways to stay well.

In this lesson, you and your teammates will solve a medical mystery. You will find how three friends came down with colds. Figure out what happened to each of the friends. Be ready to explain how people get colds and how people avoid colds.

Solving the Mystery

Maria, Chong, and Robert are good friends. Somehow, each of them caught a cold, and now they feel terrible.

Maria   Chong   Robert

TEAM TASK

Decide how the three friends became sick.
Then, make a team collage to show how
you think the three friends caught their
colds.

Team Jobs

Communicator

Manager

Tracker

Team Skills

Move into your teams quickly and quietly.

Speak softly.

Stay with your teams.

Take turns.

Do your jobs.

Team Supplies

1 copy of Maria's Story

1 copy of Chong's Story

1 copy of Robert's Story

1 sheet of construction paper

nontoxic glue

scissors for each teammate

a pencil for each teammate

job clips for 1 communicator, 1 manager, and 1 tracker

Directions for Solving the Mystery

Step 1

Each teammate, take one story.

Step 2

Each teammate, follow the directions on your story page. Put the pictures in order.

Read to yourself quietly. If you need to, ask for help.

Don't worry if you aren't sure about the order that things happened in your story. You can change your mind later.

Step 3

Take turns explaining what happened in each story.

Listen closely to one another's stories. Listen for clues that will help you solve the mystery.

Step 4

Decide how the three friends caught the colds.

Make sure that everyone agrees.

Step 5

Cut out the pictures in each story.

Step 6

Glue the pictures onto construction paper to show how the team thinks the three friends became sick.

Remember to take turns!

This will be the team's collage.

Step 7

On the back of the collage, explain how the team thinks the three friends caught their colds.

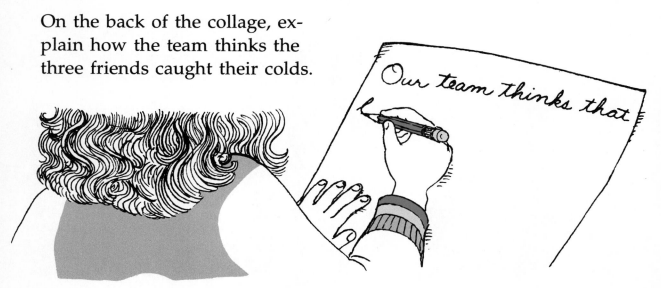

Our team thinks that

Step 8

On the back of the collage, explain how each of the three friends could have stayed well.

Make sure everyone can explain the collage and the team's answers.

Step 9

Clean up your team's workstation.

Make sure to pick up scraps of paper from the floor.

Wrap-up

Discuss these questions with your classmates.

1. What was the problem your team solved in "Solving the Mystery"?

55

2. What interactions occurred in the stories of Maria, Chong, and Robert?

3. What are the parts of the system in "Solving the Mystery"?

4. What name would you give the system in this lesson?

5. How could you keep from catching a cold?

6. Which team skill seems easiest for you to practice? Why?

7. Which team skill seems hardest for you to practice? Why?

Other Medical Mysteries

You just solved a medical mystery—how Maria, Chong, and Robert got sick. People often have to solve medical mysteries. To do so, they study the problem and look for clues that will help them explain why something happens. Once they know why it happens, people can try to fix the problem and prevent it from happening again.

Here's the story of a medical mystery that happened in Pennsylvania. The story was first printed in National Geographic World. *As you read, think about how the people solved the problem. Could this same problem happen in your town?*

The Case of the Invisible Radon

Central Control Room

◄ RADIATION DETECTOR

Date: 1984
Place: Pennsylvania

An alarm sounds as Stanley Watras, an engineer at a nuclear power plant, arrives at work. The radiation detector signals that he has been contaminated by radioactivity. How is that possible? His coworkers pass through the detectors with no problem. Watras himself works far from any radioactive materials. At first, Watras is not worried. But each time he enters the plant after that, he sets off the alarm.

Watras begins to suspect his home as a source of the radioactivity. Investigators test the house and learn that the radioactivity comes from radon gas inside it. The gas has risen from the soil beneath the house. Scientists had known that radon gas existed in uranium mines and in houses built with products of uranium mining, such as stone bearing uranium. Now they learn that the gas can also rise naturally from soil rich in uranium.

Radon forms when uranium, a chemical element in rock, decays in soil. Outside, the air spreads radon out. But when radon becomes trapped in a home, it can build up in the air. Radon may enter a home through floor drains and cracks in basement walls and floors.

Scientists know that high levels of radon may cause lung cancer. They don't know how high the levels must be before becoming dangerous. But they can determine what level is cause for concern. In the Watras home, the radon had gone *above* that level.

The Watrases moved to other housing for six months while experts sealed the house against the radon. Meanwhile, worried neighbors checked their own homes. Surprisingly, many had low radon levels. Experts learned that radon can be confined to a small area of earth. One house may be affected while the house next door is not. At last the Watrases returned to their radon-free home. They have continued to test its radon levels often.

The federal Environmental Protection Agency suggests that people call their state office of environmental protection to learn how to measure radon levels at home. High levels can be lowered by sealing cracks, by ventilating basements, or sometimes by opening windows around the house.

LESSON 6

A Music System

Why did K.T. call the band a music system? Do you think it fits the definition of a system?

Each instrument is also a system. Each has parts that interact to make a sound. When something that is part of one system is itself a system, the part can be called a subsystem. Each instrument in the band is a subsystem of the band system.

Make and Analyze
a Music System

Each person in your class will make a musical instrument. After you analyze the system, you might want to make a larger musical system by joining with your classmates and forming a band.

Supplies

3 rubber bands of different sizes

a plastic cup

paper and pencil

goggles

On Your Own

Step 1

Put on your goggles.

Step 2

Put the rubber bands over the cup as shown.

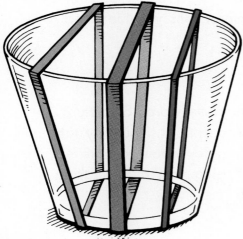

Step 3

Figure out how to use the cup-and-rubber-band system to make a sound.

Step 4

Analyze your music-making system.
- Observe the system and notice what happens.
- Ask some questions about what happens.
- Find evidence of interactions.

SAFETY CAUTION: Hold on to the rubber bands as you stretch them. Do not let them shoot across the room.

Once you can use it to make a sound, you have a music-making system.

What changes?

- Identify all the parts of the
  system.
- Answer your questions.

Use your observations and the parts
and interactions you identified.

Step 5

Write your analysis.

You may use words or pictures in
your descriptions. You may take off
your goggles when you are no
longer using your music-making
system.

Step 6

Write answers to the Wrap-up
questions.

Write your answers to these questions on the
same page as your analysis of the music system.

1. Is a guitar a system? Why or why not?

2. What is an example of two objects interacting?

3. Which objects would you include in a
   system in order to answer one of the
   questions on the next page? Choose one
   question.

(Remember, limiting what you look at makes studying the system easier.)

a. How can I make a kite fly higher?

b. How can I use a computer to play a game?

c. How can I make the sound of a drum lower?

d. Make up your own question.

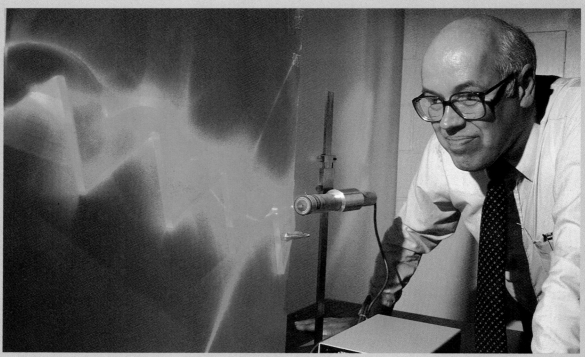

UNIT 2

Interactions and Variables
SYSTEMS AND ANALYSIS IN SCIENCE

Introduction

K.T. and C.Q. are trying to find out about systems in their world. The more they find out about systems, the better they will understand how things work together in the world around them. When they learn about new things, K.T. and C.Q. like to work together. They know that when they work together, they can come up with many more ideas and answers than when they work alone.

In this unit, you will be finding out more about systems, too. You might know about some of the systems you will study, but others might be new to you. Just as you did in Unit 1, you will work together with teammates. You will learn more about systems, and you will learn more about what it means to work as a team. When you work as a team, you share a lot of things—you share equipment, you share ideas, and you share the work, too.

In Unit 1, you learned to take turns in your team. What did you do in your team when you practiced the skill: **Take turns**? Was taking turns always easy to do?

One way to take turns is to share your ideas. **Share your ideas** is a new team skill your team will practice in this unit. When you share your ideas, you take turns talking. You also take turns listening. You learn new things from one another when you share your ideas.

You can practice this new skill by saying things such as the following:

- "What do you think about this question?"

- "I am not sure about this. What do you think?"

- "You have not given us your idea yet. Please tell us what you think."

- "We need to agree on one team answer. Let's all give one suggestion, and then we can decide which answer is best."

- "I do not agree. This is what I think."

Sharing your ideas is not always easy, but you can usually come up with more and better answers when you put your heads together. Try practicing this skill every time you work as a team. Remember, everyone has good ideas to share. It is your team's responsibility to be sure everyone has a chance to share ideas.

LESSON 7 Nondivers

In an earlier lesson, you used analysis to solve the case of the sick friends. You figured out how the friends got sick, and then you thought of ways the friends might have prevented themselves from becoming sick. In this lesson, you will see if you understand another system well enough to prevent something from happening.

How well do you understand the bottle-diver system? With your teammates, see if you can change the bottle-diver system so that a dropper will not dive when you squeeze the bottle.

Changing the System

Each team's challenge in this lesson is to change the bottle-diver system so that it contains two droppers. One of the droppers should dive when you squeeze the bottle. The other dropper should not dive when you squeeze the bottle.

TEAM TASK

Change your team's bottle-diver system from Lesson 4 so one dropper does not "dive" when you squeeze the bottle. The other dropper should still "dive."

Team Skill

Share your ideas.

Team Jobs

 Communicator

 Manager

 Tracker

Team Supplies

1 bottle-diver system from Lesson 4

1 dropper

job clips for 1 communicator, 1 manager, and 1 tracker

Directions for Changing the System

Step 1

Decide what change you want to make in the bottle-diver system so you can complete the team task.

Which parts of the bottle-diver system could you change to complete the team task? How could you change each part? What materials could you use to make the changes?

Step 2

MANAGER: Go to the supply table and get the supplies your team decides to use.

Only the manager goes to the supply table, but the whole team decides what the manager should get.

CAUTION

Step 3

Make the change.

Wipe up spilled water right away.

Step 4

Test the bottle diver to see if
the team has completed the
team task.

Observe what happens. The first dropper should "dive." The second one
should not.

Step 5

Decide whether you completed
the task.

If not, decide what you want to do
next. Do it, if you have enough time.

Systems and Analysis

People analyze systems for a number of
reasons. Sometimes, they want to learn more
about the system.

Sometimes, they want to repair a system that is broken.

Sometimes, they want to improve a system.

Sometimes, they want to solve a problem.

Usually, when people repair a system, improve a system, or solve a problem in a system, they learn more about the system, too. For example, your team had a problem to solve. Your problem was how to prevent a dropper from diving when you squeezed a bottle. To solve the problem, your team decided which parts of the system to change.

When you changed a part of your system and observed what happened, you learned more about how your system worked. Once you understood more about the system, you could then make changes that would solve a certain problem or answer a certain question. The process of analysis your team might have used in solving the problem is shown in the box.

A Process of Analysis

- Ask a question or identify a problem.

- Observe the system.

- Describe the evidence that parts of the system are interacting.

- Identify the parts of the system.

- Change a part of the system.

- Observe the changed system and look for differences.

- Answer the question or solve the problem.

While you were trying to complete the team task, your team probably asked questions such as these:

- What will happen if we change the amount of water in the dropper?

- What will happen if we block the hole in the dropper?

- What will happen if we change how hard we squeeze the bottle?

To answer the team's questions, you changed your bottle-diver system in some way. Then, you observed the new system, and you learned more about how the system worked. When you had learned enough, you could solve your problem.

Wrap-up

With your teammates, agree on answers to these questions. Write the team's answers on one sheet of paper. Be ready to share your answers with the class.

1. What problem was your team trying to solve when you changed the system?

2. What is one question your team asked and answered as you changed the bottle-diver system?

3. Why did you make the change you did?

4. After you changed the bottle-diver system, was it still a system? Why or why not?

5. What are two things your team did to use the team skill: **Share your ideas**?

Which One Would You Buy?

Have you ever bought something you were disappointed with later? If so, you're not alone. Advertisements make every product look good. Sometimes, the products do what you want them to, and, other times, the products don't. Is there any way to know the difference before you spend your money?

There is a way to find out about a product before you buy it. Some magazines, such as *Consumer Reports* and *Zillions* (formerly *Penny Power*), analyze products and report the results of the analysis for you. You can read the report and decide whether the product will work for you.

Here is an analysis that the magazine Zillions did of two pocket video games. As you read the analysis, think about these questions:

- *What parts of the video systems did Zillions report about?*

- *What questions did the magazine ask about each of the parts?*

- *How did the magazine answer each of the questions?*

- *Would reading this analysis help you decide whether to buy one of the video systems? Why or why not?*

Lynx vs *Game Boy*

One is black. One is gray. How else do these two small video game systems differ? Nine video game fans spent weeks finding out.

Thanks to our testers: Kenneth Applebaum, New York, New York; Debbie, Lauren and Robby Berliner, Greenbaugh, New York; Jacob and Spencer Hutchings, Larchmont, New York; Andrew Jenter, Salisbury, Connecticut; William Shubert, Honolulu, Hawaii; Anson Tripp, Amherst, Massachusetts.

Start Up

Are they easy to learn? A snap, said our testers. Game Boy and Lynx both work like mini-Nintendo systems. Just pop in a tiny cartridge and start fingering the familiar controls. Lynx may take a smidge more effort to master, but no one reported major problems getting going with either system.

Winner: **a tie**

Graphics

How exciting are the images? The video screens are both quite small. So color is the key. Game Boy's graphics are black and boring gray. Lynx's are bright and colorful. Lynx has lots of computer memory, so its images are sharp and detailed. "In some games they look better than Nintendo," said Andrew. Our testers rated the Lynx graphics "excellent."

In comparison, Game Boy characters and backgrounds look primitive. Most testers found the screen hard to see unless it was held at the perfect angle. Game Boy earned a lukewarm "okay" rating for graphics.

Winner: **Lynx**

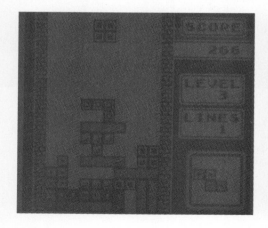 

Sound Effects

Which has super sounds? Neither system would get Paula Abdul up on the dance floor. Both pipe out perky little background tunes, however, and Lauren found herself humming Game Boy music in the shower. But most agreed with William: "The Lynx sound tracks are more detailed and amusing." Lynx's extra sound effects delighted Kenneth: "You can actually hear your BMX bike get bent out of shape!"

Game Boy comes with a little set of earphones. And it should, according to most testers. "The sound is so soft you really need the earphones to hear it," warned William.

Winner: Lynx

Convenience

Is one system easier to use? When it comes to controls, no. Both have familiar, Nintendo-like fingertip buttons. When it comes to portability, yes. Game Boy is hand-held and pocket-sized. You'll need a backpack to tote your laptop Lynx. They differ on power use as well. Game Boy's four AA batteries provide a generous 10 hours of play. Lynx runs through its six AA's in just a few hours. Luckily, Lynx comes with a power adaptor to plug into an electrical outlet.

Both Game Boy and Lynx come with linking cables so you and your buddy can compete against each other. However, each player must have a system and cartridge. Lynx allows left-handers to flip the image for easier play.

Overall, our testers preferred Game Boy's pick-up-and-go convenience. "You can take it anywhere," said Debbie. Lynx's size and battery drain make it more suitable for home play.

Winner: *Game Boy*

Games

Does one system have better games? Each comes with one game cartridge. Our testers also tried three additional games for each system.

Game Boy comes with the Soviet-designed game, *Tetris*. Andrew thought this block-building game was "fun and addicting." William found it the most challenging of all the games because of its increasing difficulty. Anson said *Super Mario Land* was more playable than the Nintendo versions, despite poor graphics. On the other hand, *Tennis* ("blah") and *Boxxle* ("what's the point?") bombed with the testers.

Spencer and others liked just two of the four *California Games* on the cartridge that came with the Lynx system: surfing and BMX racing. Three other cartridges (*Blue Lightning*, *Gates of Zendocon*, and *Chip's Challenge*) were fun and challenging for most testers.

Both systems have good and so-so games available. New games for both are due to be released soon.

Winner: a tie

Cost

Is one system kinder to your wallet? We paid a whopping $180 for Lynx. (That's more than standard Nintendo and Sega systems.) Games cost an additional $35 each. In contrast, Game Boy is about half the price, at $90 for the system and $20 for games.

Winner: *Game Boy*

Down to the Wire

Did all that make you greedy for a Game Boy? Long for a Lynx? That's what we asked our nine testers at the end of their try-out period. Reactions were mixed.

Kenneth and Jacob said Lynx outperformed Game Boy because of better "color, sharpness, and sound." Spencer and Lauren thought about convenience and cost and decided that "Game Boy wins overall." Andrew and Robby couldn't choose because "they're both lots of fun to play."

But three testers weren't crazy about either system. Anson complained that "playing with them can kill you if you've got lots of homework." Debbie didn't like the cost: "That's a lot of money to pay for anything, and they aren't that special." William said, "I'd rather own something I wouldn't become bored with in two weeks."

So who won? You will, if you think twice before buying either system. Andrew admitted, "I liked both, but I wouldn't spend my own money on them. You'd do better buying regular Nintendo games."

Analyzing Antacids

Pretend that one of the consumer magazines asked your team to help analyze two products. Use what you know about systems and analysis to help you test the products. Be ready to report the results of your analysis so others can decide which product they would prefer to buy.

On the next page are advertisements that describe the two products you will analyze. The products are called **antacids**. Antacids are a type of medicine.

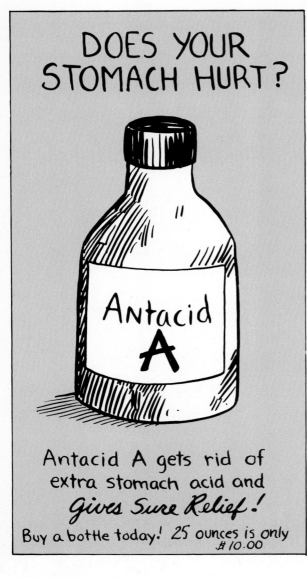

DOES YOUR STOMACH HURT?

Antacid A

Antacid A gets rid of extra stomach acid and *Gives Sure Relief!*

Buy a bottle today! 25 ounces is only $10.00

Is A Pain in Your Stomach

Causing a Pain In Your Wallet?

Antacid B

Gets rid of extra stomach acid and saves you money $$!

Take less of Antacid B than you take of the other brands. 25 ounces costs only $15.00.

TAKE LESS, SAVE MORE!

In your stomach, acids mix with food you eat. Acids help break the food into parts your body can use. Sometimes, however, people have too much acid in their stomachs. Then, they might feel pain in their stomachs. To get rid of the extra acid, some people take antacids when they have stomach pain. If too much stomach acid caused the pain, an antacid (anti-acid) could make a person feel better.

Is the claim in the ad for Antacid B true? Which antacid would you really need to take less of to get rid of extra stomach acid? You and your teammates will analyze both antacids to find out. To help you know when the antacid has gotten rid of the extra acid, you will use a chemical called BTB. By itself, BTB is dark blue. When you mix BTB with an acid, it changes to bright yellow. When you add enough antacid to get rid of the acid, the color of the BTB changes back to blue.

In this product test, you will mix 10 drops of acid with 20 drops of BTB. Then, you will count how many drops of antacid you must add before the BTB changes back to blue. The antacid that changes the color of the BTB after fewer drops is the one you need less of to take care of the extra acid.

SAFETY CAUTION: Wear your safety goggles during this lesson. Wash your hands when you finish.

TEAM TASK

Analyze two antacids to find out which one you need less of to take care of extra stomach acid.

Team Jobs

Communicator

Manager

Tracker

Team Skill

Share your ideas.

Team Supplies

1 copy of Product Testing Record Page

1 tray

2 medicine cups, each filled with 10 drops of acid and 20 drops of BTB

1 medicine cup, covered with a lid, filled with 20 drops of BTB

1 bottle of Antacid A (shared with other teams)

1 bottle of Antacid B (shared with other teams)

safety goggles for each teammate

pencils

job clips for 1 communicator, 1 manager, and 1 tracker

Directions for Analyzing Antacids

Step 1

Get a bottle of Antacid A or Antacid B.

Your team will need to share these bottles with other teams. It does not matter which antacid the team tests first.

Step 2

Add one drop of the antacid to **one** of the medicine cups filled with BTB and acid.

Take turns so that every teammate does a part.

One teammate might add the drops. Another teammate might swirl the cup. The third teammate might count how many drops of antacid it takes before the color changes.

Step 3

Mix the antacid with the acid and BTB by gently swirling the medicine cup.

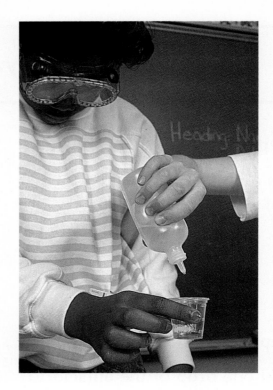

Step 4

Keep adding drops of antacid and swirling the cup until the color changes to blue and stays blue.

To help you decide when the color has changed to blue, compare the color in this cup with the color in the cup filled with just BTB.

Step 5

On the record page, write down how many drops of the antacid it took to take care of the acid.

Step 6

Repeat these steps for the other antacid.

Start with another cup of BTB and acid.

Step 7

Agree on answers to the questions on the record page.

Step 8

On the record page, write down the team's answers to the questions.

Wrap-up

Discuss these questions with your classmates.

1. Which antacid do you need less of to take care of extra stomach acid? How do you know?

2. Was your test of the antacids a fair test? Why do you think so?

3. How could analyzing a product help people decide whether to buy the product?

LESSON 9

What Will Happen If . . . ?

C.Q. and K.T. analyzed a marble-racing system. They observed what happened when they raced two glass marbles down the ramp. C.Q. timed how long it took for the marbles to roll down the ramp, and K.T. measured how far the marbles rolled past the end of the ramp. They recorded the measurements as part of their analysis of the system.

C.Q. and K.T. weren't satisfied with their system. They wanted the marbles to roll faster and farther than before, but they weren't sure how to do it.

To solve their problem, C.Q. and K.T. decided to analyze their system some more. They decided to change some parts of the system and see how the changes affected how far or how fast the marbles rolled. C.Q. and K.T. wondered how three different changes might affect what happened. They asked these questions:

- What will happen if we race bigger marbles?

- What will happen if we change the surface of the ramp?

- What will happen if we change the height of the ramp?

Fair Tests

To find out the answer to each question, C.Q. and K.T. needed to do some testing. C.Q. and K.T. set up three fair tests, one test for each question. In each fair test, they changed one part of the system. Then, they remeasured how fast and how far the marbles rolled. By comparing the new measurements to the measurements they made earlier, C.Q. and K.T. would know whether the changes had an effect on the system.

Here is how they set up each fair test.

Fair Test 1

Question: What will happen if we race bigger marbles?

C.Q. and K.T. replaced the marbles with two larger ones, but they kept everything else about the ramp the same as before. They measured the results carefully.

Fair Test 2

Question: What will happen if we change the surface of the ramp?

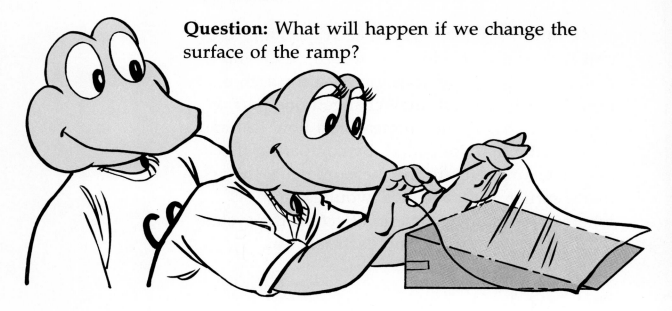

C.Q. and K.T. used the two smaller marbles, but they covered the surface of the ramp with wax paper to make it smoother. They measured again.

Fair Test 3

Question: What will happen if we change the height of the ramp?

C.Q. and K.T. removed the wax paper, but they made the ramp much higher than before. They raced the two small marbles and measured again.

With your classmates, discuss these questions about the three fair tests.

- What change did C.Q. and K.T. make for each fair test?

- What did they keep the same for each fair test?

- Why didn't C.Q. and K.T. make more than one change for each test?

- How do you think each change affected how fast or how far the marbles rolled?

Testing Variables

When C.Q. and K.T. made changes in the system to see what would happen, they were testing **variables.** (To **vary** means to change. So **variable** means changeable. A **variable** is something that you change about a system or something that changes as a result of the change you make.) What variable did C.Q. and K.T. test in each fair test?

C.Q. and K.T. tested one variable in the system at a time. By testing only one variable, they could observe what effect that variable had on interactions in the system.

For example, in the first test, C.Q. and K.T. tested the variable of size of the marble. To make the test fair, C.Q. and K.T. used larger marbles but kept everything else about the system the same as before. If the results of this test showed that the marbles rolled faster and farther than before, C.Q. and K.T. would know more about how the variable of size of the marble affects the system.

This doesn't mean that marble size is the **only** variable that affects how fast and how far the marbles roll. C.Q. and K.T. tested other variables to see if the height of the ramp or the surface of the ramp also made a difference. After their tests, C.Q. and K.T. might have decided to make several changes in the system all at once to make the marbles roll the fastest and farthest.

Earlier in this unit, you set up some fair tests. In Lesson 7 you tested variables in a bottle-diver system. In Lesson 8 you tested variables in an antacid system.

Think about the variables you tested in each of those lessons. Discuss the following questions with your classmates:

- Were the tests fair?

- What variables did you test?

- What evidence did you have that the variables changed what happened in the systems?

Analyzing a Floating Ping-Pong Ball System

Your teacher will show you a floating Ping-Pong ball system. With your teammates, you will analyze the system. Then, the team will ask one "What will happen if . . . ?" question about the system.

Plan a fair test that would help the team find the answer to the question. Identify the **variable** you will test. Also explain how you would know whether that variable affects what happens in the system. Be ready to explain your team's fair test to the rest of the class. Your teacher will help the class set up several fair tests and find out what happens.

TEAM TASK

Analyze a floating Ping-Pong ball system. Design a fair test of one variable in this system. Identify the variable. Decide how you will know whether the variable affects what happens in the system.

Team Skill

Share your ideas.

Team Jobs

Communicator

Tracker

Checker

Team Supplies

1 sheet of paper and a pencil

job clips for 1 communicator, 1 tracker, and
1 checker

Directions for Analyzing a
Floating Ping-Pong Ball System

Step 1

Observe the system.

On the sheet of paper, record the
team's observations.

Step 2

Describe evidence that parts of
the system are interacting.

On the sheet of paper, write down
the evidence.

Take turns writing. Make
sure everyone shares ideas.

Step 3

Identify the parts of the system.

On the paper, list the parts.

Step 4

Ask one "What will happen if . . . ?" question the team would like to answer about this system.

Write down the question. If the team needs help asking "What will happen if . . . ?" questions, reread pages 97–101 about C.Q. and K.T.'s fair tests.

Step 5

Plan a fair test for the team's "What will happen if . . . ?" question.

Use words or pictures to describe the test.

Step 6

Write why the test is a fair test.

Step 7

Identify the variable the team will test.

Do you remember what a variable is? If not, reread "Testing Variables" on pages 101–102.

Step 8

Decide how you will know
whether the variable affects
what happens in the system.

Write what evidence the team will
look for.

Step 9

Sign the paper to show that
you each can explain what the
team wrote.

Write the answers to these questions on your
own paper.

1. What is a fair test?

2. What is a variable?

3. How could a fair test help you find out
   whether a variable affects what happens in
   a system?

LESSON **10** Moldy Oldies

In this lesson, you will grow something that you might have seen before. You might have seen it on bread, on food in the refrigerator, on pieces of fruit, even on fish food at the bottom of an aquarium. That something is mold. Can you remember places you have seen mold growing? What did the mold look like?

Yuck! There's green stuff in here!

Describing Mold

Today, you will look closely at some moldy bread. Later, you and your teammates will grow mold on your own pieces of bread.

TEAM TASK

Examine a piece of moldy bread in a sealed plastic bag. Describe what you observe.

Team Jobs

 Communicator

 Manager

 Tracker

Team Skills

Share your ideas.

Team Supplies

1 slice of moldy bread in a plastic bag

3 hand lenses

3 sheets of drawing paper

crayons

paper and pencils

job clips for 1 communicator, 1 manager, and 1 tracker

Directions for Describing Mold

Step 1

Look closely at the moldy bread inside the plastic bag.

SAFETY CAUTION: When observing the mold, do not open the plastic bag or take the bread out of the bag. Some people are allergic to mold. Breathing what is in the bag could make them sick. If you know you are allergic to molds, let your teacher know.

Use your hand lens and take turns.

Step 2

Describe the moldy bread.

Share your ideas with your team-mates.

Step 3

Write "Record Page for Describing Mold" at the top of one sheet of lined paper.

Step 4

Write the team's description on the team's record page.

Step 5

On the sheets of drawing paper, draw pictures of the moldy bread.

Each teammate draws a picture. Show the colors of the mold and where it is on the bread. Try to make your picture look exactly like the bread in the plastic bag.

Step 6

On the team's record page, list places where teammates have seen mold.

Remember to share your ideas.

Step 7

Sign your team's record page
when you can explain what is
on the page.

Step 8

Sign your drawing and attach
all teammates' drawings to the
team's record page.

Mold-growing Systems

Today, it's your turn to grow some mold. The
mold you grow might look like the mold on the
slice of bread you observed, or it might not.
There are many different kinds of mold.

To grow mold, you won't need to go to the
store for seeds. The air is full of mold "seeds,"
which are called spores. Spores are really not
seeds at all. They are different from seeds in
many ways.

Spores can stay alive for long periods of time
in places that are very hot and in places that are
very dry. In those same places, most seeds
would die and would not be able to grow into a
plant. Mold spores are very hardy. They stay dor-
mant—in a resting or waiting state—until the
conditions are right. Then, spores grow like
crazy!

Another difference between spores and seeds is that seeds contain a supply of food that helps a plant begin to grow. Spores carry no food with them. Spores use whatever they land on as food. Also, seeds are very big compared with spores. Spores are nearly invisible. People usually do not know that spores are around until the spores land on something and start to grow into mold.

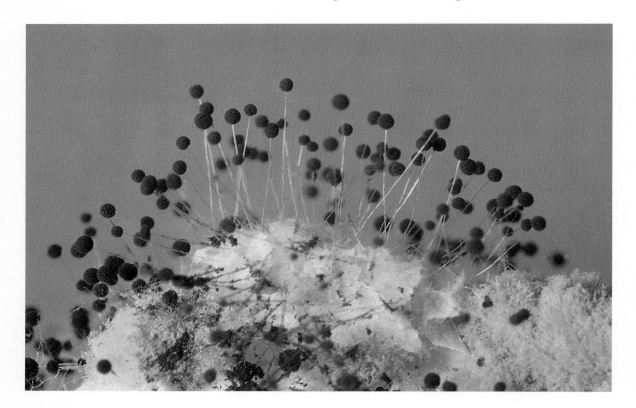

Making Mold-growing Systems

Your challenge in making mold-growing systems is to find out what molds need in order to grow. First, you will share your ideas as a class. What do you think helps molds grow? Your answers to this question become the variables you will test. Then, teams will make their own mold-growing systems. Each team will test different variables to find out what molds need in order to grow.

As the molds grow, your team will check its mold-growing systems each day and record any evidence that interactions have taken place. Don't be impatient, though. Molds won't grow overnight. You will have to wait about a week before your mold-growing systems grow some mold.

After a week, you will decide what helped the molds to grow. The teams that have grown the best, the most colorful, and the ugliest molds will receive Champion Mold Growers' Awards!

TEAM TASK

Make three mold-growing systems and three record pages. (Each mold-growing system will test one variable for growing molds.) Observe your systems and record your observations.

Team Jobs

Communicator   Manager   Tracker

Team Skill

Share your ideas.

Team Supplies

1 1/2 slices of bread

3 resealable plastic bags

masking tape

paper and pencils

job clips for 1 communicator, 1 manager,
and 1 tracker

Directions for Making
Mold-growing Systems

Step 1

Decide on a good name for a
bunch of mold growers. This
will be your official team name.

Step 2

Decide on three "What will happen if . . . ?" questions the team wants to answer about mold-growing systems.

Share your ideas.

Step 3

Plan how to test the variable in each "What will happen if . . . ?" question.

The team will make three mold-growing systems, one for each teammate. Each system should test one variable.

SAFETY CAUTION: You may not test variables that would grow mold outside the plastic bags. Someone might get sick by breathing the mold spores.

Step 4

Explain your questions and your plans to your teacher before you go on to Step 5.

Step 5

Pick up your team's supplies.

Remember, the manager picks up and returns all supplies.

Step 6

Place masking tape on each plastic bag. Write your team's name and the "What will happen if . . . ?" question on the piece of masking tape.

Step 7

Set up your team's mold-growing systems.

Use one-half slice of bread and one plastic bag in each system.

Step 8

Each teammate, make a record page that looks like this.

Each teammate will keep track of one mold-growing system.

Record Page

Name of our team: _____

My name: _____

What will happen if _____

_____ ?

My observations:

Day	Description of Bread
1	
2	
3	
4	
5	
6	
7	

Step 9

Check the team's mold-growing systems each day for the next week. Record the team's observations for the mold-growing system you are keeping track of.

Step 10

On the last day of your observations, rate the team's mold-growing systems. Use a scale from 1 to 3: 1 = no mold, 2 = some mold, and 3 = lots of mold.

Discussion Questions

As a class, decide on answers to the following.

1. What helps mold grow?

2. What keeps mold from growing?

3. What is a system that would grow lots of mold?

4. What is a system that would grow little or no mold?

Solving a Mold-growing Problem

You now know a lot about a mold-growing system. You have observed the system. You have described evidence that parts of the system are interacting. You have identified the parts of the system. You have changed parts of the system and looked for differences in what happened to the system. In other words, you have analyzed a mold-growing system.

To see how well your team understands a mold-growing system, you will predict what conditions will create the moldiest bread and what conditions will keep the bread freshest. Then, you'll test your predictions.

TEAM TASK

Make a mold-growing system that will grow a lot of mold. Make a mold-growing system that will not grow any mold. Test your systems.

Team Jobs

 Communicator

 Manager

 Tracker

Team Skill

Share your ideas.

Team Supplies

1 slice of bread

2 resealable plastic bags

masking tape

paper and pencils

job clips for 1 communicator, 1 manager,
and 1 tracker

Directions for Solving a Mold-growing Problem

Step 1

Predict what conditions will
make a lot of mold grow on
the bread.

Use the results of your class's
analysis of the mold-growing systems.
Share your ideas before you make
your predictions.

Step 2

Record your predictions for
growing a lot of mold.

Make your own record page for
recording your predictions.

Step 3

Predict what conditions will keep the bread fresh.

That means you don't want any mold to grow on it. Share your ideas before you make your predictions.

Step 4

Record your predictions for keeping the bread fresh.

Step 5

Pick up the supplies, put a piece of masking tape on each plastic bag, and label each bag.

Label each bag with your team's name. Write "moldy" on one bag and "fresh" on the other.

Step 6

Test your team's predictions by setting up two systems. Make one system that will grow a lot of mold and another that will not grow any mold.

You might want to change more than one part of each system this time.

Step 7

On your record page, write the problem you are trying to solve in each mold-growing system.

Step 8

Identify the parts of each system.

On your record page, record the parts.

Step 9

Describe the changes you made in each system.

Be ready to tell the class why your team made those changes. Be sure everyone on the team can explain why.

Step 10

Observe the systems each day, and look for any differences in what happens.

Step 11

Each day, record your observations of each system.

Your team can decide how you want to record your observations. You might write about your results or draw pictures or do both.

Wrap-up

After one week, write a team report about your investigation. Use the following questions to help you write your report.

1. What problems did your team try to solve?

2. How did you set up your systems to solve each problem?

3. Did you solve the problems? Why or why not?

4. What did your team learn about mold-growing systems?

5. What would your team do differently next time?

6. In what ways did sharing your ideas help with the team task?

A Breathing System

You can think of your body as a system. It has parts that interact with one another and with the outside world. You can also think of different parts of your body as systems. Maybe you've heard of some of these systems—the digestive system and the nervous system are two of them. Today, you will analyze the body system that you use for breathing. It is called the respiratory system.

I'll huff and I'll puff and I'll use my respiratory system to blow your house down!

Making a Model of the Respiratory System

In Lesson 3, you learned that a system is a group of objects that interact. If your respiratory system is called a system, it must be made of parts that interact. Have you ever wondered what those parts are? How can you find out how those parts interact? After all, it would be pretty difficult to study your own respiratory system or the respiratory system of your classmates.

What can you do if you want to learn about a system that you cannot observe? One way you can learn about a system is to make a model of it. Then, you can study the model to learn about the real system. In this activity, your team will make a model of the respiratory system.

TEAM TASK

Make a model of the respiratory system. Analyze the model and explain your evidence that the parts interact.

Team Jobs

Communicator

Manager

Tracker

Team Skill

Share your ideas.

Team Supplies

1 clear plastic cup with a hole in the bottom

1 plastic straw

1 large balloon

1 small balloon

scissors

safety goggles for each teammate

masking tape

paper and pencils

job clips for 1 communicator, 1 manager, and 1 tracker

Directions for Making a Model of the Respiratory System

Step 1

Put on your safety goggles.

Step 2

Put the small balloon over one end of the straw. Tape the balloon tightly to the straw.

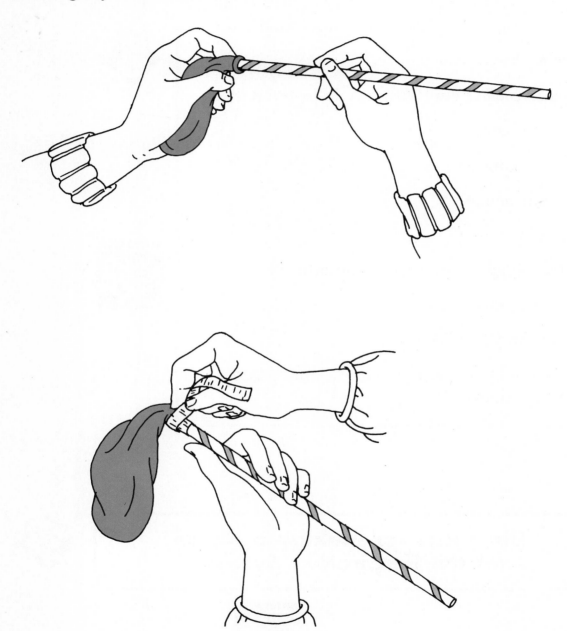

Step 3

Turn the cup upside-down and put the straw through the hole in the bottom of the cup so the balloon is inside the cup.

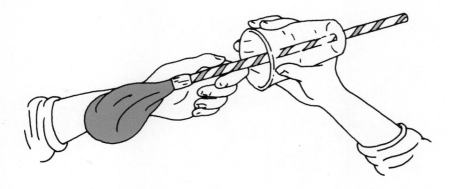

Step 4

Pull the straw through the hole so the small balloon hangs inside the plastic cup. Tape the straw to the cup.

Be sure everyone gets a turn to do something while you are making the model.

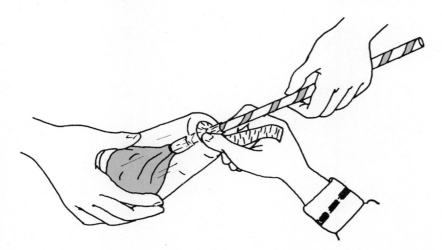

Step 5

Cut the narrow part (the part
you blow through) off the large
balloon. Stretch out the bottom
part of the balloon so it lies flat.

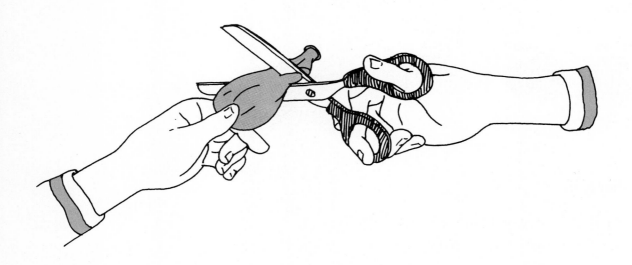

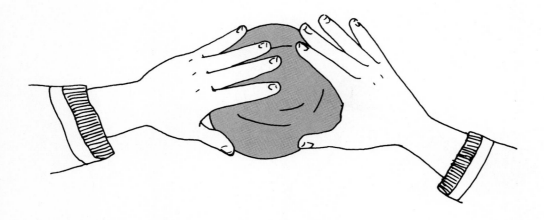

Step 6

Stretch the piece of rubber
from the large balloon over the
wide, open part of the cup. Use
masking tape to tape this piece
of rubber tightly to the cup.

Be sure you tape the piece of rubber
tightly so it cannot fall off or be
pulled off the cup.

Step 7

Use the model of the respiratory system by pulling down
on the piece of rubber balloon.

Take turns pulling down on the piece
of rubber balloon. Share your observations.

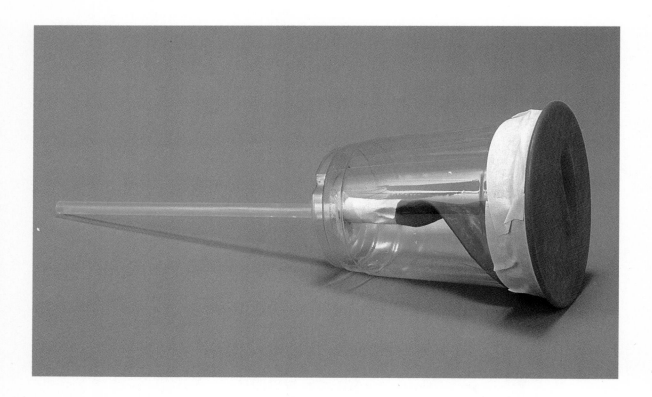

Step 8

Decide on team answers to the
Discussion Questions.

Be ready to share the team's
answers with the class.

Step 9

Analyze the model of the
respiratory system.
- Observe the model.
- Describe evidence that parts
  of the model are interacting.
- Identify the parts of the
  model.

Discussion Questions

1. How is the model like your own
   respiratory system?

2. How is the model different from your own
   respiratory system?

3. Is the model also a system? Why or why
   not?

Becoming an Expert on the Respiratory System

You made a model of the respiratory system
because you could not observe someone's
respiratory system directly. There is another way
you can learn about a system that you cannot observe. You can read to find out what other
people, such as doctors, have learned about the
respiratory system by observing it.

In this activity, you and your teammates will each become an expert about part of the respiratory system. Then, each of you will share with your teammates what you have learned. By sharing your knowledge, you will all know a lot about how the respiratory system works.

TEAM TASK

Share information from fact sheets about the respiratory system. Analyze the respiratory system using the information on the fact sheets and your model of the respiratory system.

Team Jobs

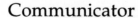

| Communicator | Checker | Tracker |

Team Skill

Share your ideas.

Team Supplies

3 fact sheets about the respiratory system

paper and pencils

your team's model of the respiratory system

job clips for 1 communicator, 1 checker,
and 1 tracker

Directions for Becoming an Expert on the Respiratory System

Step 1

Meet with classmates who have the same team job you have.

All the communicators will meet in one group, all the checkers in another, and all the trackers in another.

Step 2

Read your fact sheet on the respiratory system.

You will become an expert on the fact sheet you have.

Step 3

Move back into your team, and, one at a time, share the information on each teammate's fact sheet.

You can decide who will share first. The order for sharing the information does not matter.

Step 4

As a team, analyze the respiratory system.

- Describe evidence of interactions in the respiratory system.
- List the parts of the system.

You can write about the evidence of interactions or draw pictures that show the interactions. You can also use your model to demonstrate some of the interactions you read about.

Step 5

When each member of your team agrees with the team's analysis, sign the paper to show that you agree.

Save your analysis to share with the class.

What Will Happen If . . . ?

Once you know a lot about a system, you can make predictions about what might happen if changes take place in the system. Remember when you wrote answers to "What will happen if . . . ?" questions about a floating Ping-Pong ball system and mold-growing systems? When you were studying those systems, you could change variables in the system and watch what happened.

In this lesson, you cannot observe the system you are studying—the respiratory system—but you can still make predictions using "What will happen if . . . ?" questions. You can make predictions because you have learned a lot about the respiratory system by making a model, by reading, and by sharing your ideas.

TEAM TASK

Predict the answers to "What will happen if . . . ?" questions about the respiratory system.

Team Jobs

You will not need team jobs for this task.

Directions for What Will Happen If . . . ?

Step 1

Read each of the "What will happen if . . . ?" questions below.

The questions describe variables in the respiratory system.

A: What will happen if someone's nose is plugged so the person cannot use it for breathing?

B: What will happen if something that does not let oxygen or carbon dioxide pass coats the air sacs in the lungs?

C: What will happen if the mucus and tiny hairs in the nasal passages are removed?

D: What will happen if a paper bag is put over a person's mouth and nose?

E: What will happen if a person breathes air that does not have much oxygen in it?

F: What will happen if the air sacs are removed from the lungs?

Step 2

Using your team's model and your analysis of the respiratory system, predict the answer to each "What will happen if . . . ?" question in Step 1.

Decide whether the changes will affect any important interactions in the system.

Step 3

Write your team's predictions on a piece of paper.

Be sure you share ideas before you write your team's predictions.

Step 4

Be ready to explain your team's predictions.

Each member of your team should be able to explain the team's predictions.

The team skill in Unit 2 is **share your ideas.** On your own paper, explain some ways your team shared ideas in this and other lessons.

This article is from Current Health, *May 1990. As you read the article, think about how you can take care of your respiratory system and why that is important.*

It's Breath-taking!

The Respiratory System

Breathing is the first thing you do when you're born and it doesn't stop until you die. You can hold your breath. You can take deep breaths. But most of the time breathing is so automatic you never even think about it. If you do pay attention to your breathing, you may be surprised to learn that you breathe more than 21,000 times every day! . . .

Your Air Supply

Did you know that you use about 5,000 gallons of air every day? Most of the air is a gas called *nitrogen* (nī´–trə–jən). About one-fifth of the air you breathe in is oxygen; about one-hundredth is carbon dioxide.

You don't use all the oxygen you take in. Some of it is still in the air you breathe out. The leftover oxygen makes rescue breathing possible. That's why you can help someone who has stopped breathing. You can blow air into the person's mouth and lungs. Rescue breathing is part of CPR. The letters *CPR* stand for *cardiopulmonary resuscitation* (car–dē–ō–pul´–mə–ner–ē ri–səs–ə–tā´–shun).

The lungs are more in touch with the outside air than is any other part of the body, even more than the skin. If you could spread out the space in your lungs, it would take up 40 times more space than the area covered by your skin! If 40 students your size stood together, the total amount of space used by everyone's skin would be about the same as the space inside one person's lungs. That's why clean air is so important.

But air has more than nitrogen, oxygen, and carbon dioxide in it. Air is also full of dirt and germs. The dirt and germs can hurt the respiratory system. . . .

Sneezes and Wheezes

The lungs are able to protect themselves from dirt and germs in the air. If something blocks or irritates your airways, you can sneeze or cough. The lining of the lungs and the nose traps dirt. Tiny hairs beat back and forth. They send the dirt back to the throat. Sometimes dirt or germs get through to the air spaces. Groups of large white cells eat or remove dirt and germs so they can't hurt you.

The lungs can't keep everything out. That's often why you get sick. Have you ever had a cold or the flu? These illnesses are caused by germs that attack the lungs. A cold may be caused by any of 200 different *viruses* (vī´-rəs-əs). There are many different kinds of flu, too.

Be Good to Your Respiratory System

Other diseases can hurt the respiratory system. Some make breathing hard by blocking airways. Some slow down blood flow in the lungs. Others make it hard for the chest cavity to let in air. Lung cancer is one of the worst diseases of the respiratory system. Anyone who smokes has a chance of getting it. . . . You can do a lot to keep your respiratory system healthy. . . .

Stay Smoke-Free

The most important way to keep your respiratory system healthy is not to smoke. Cigarette smoke contains at least 200 different poisons. Smoking slows down or stops the movement of hairs that clean the airways. It also slows down blood flow in the lungs. It makes it hard for the blood to carry oxygen.

Smoke from someone else's cigarette, called second-hand smoke, can hurt you even if you never puff on a cigarette. Second-hand smoke has more poison than smoke from a cigarette people smoke themselves. Second-hand smoke has twice as much of the poisons tar and nicotine, and three times as much of the poison carbon monoxide. Children who live in a house with a smoker are twice as likely to get sick as children who live in a smoke-free home. The best advice is: If you don't smoke, don't start. If you do smoke, quit. . . . If you eat right, exercise, and never smoke, you'll keep your lungs and the rest of your respiratory system healthy for every breath you take.

The Television-watching System

"THE COUCH POTATO SYSTEM"

    C.Q.'s mother thinks that C.Q. sits around watching television too much. She wants her son to get more exercise. To solve this problem, C.Q.'s mother designed a new invention—she invented a television-watching system for her son to use. Here is how the television-watching system works.

Analyzing the Television-watching System

Show what you have learned about interactions and variables by analyzing the television-watching system. Work with your teammates to analyze the system. Be ready to compare your team's analysis of the system with that of other teams in your class.

TEAM TASK

Analyze the television-watching system.

Team Jobs

You will not need team jobs for this task.

Team Skill

Share your ideas.

Team Supplies

paper and pencils

Directions for Analyzing the Television-watching System

Step 1

Read each of the Wrap-up
questions.

149

Step 2

Agree on answers to each of
the questions.

Remember to share your ideas.

Step 3

Take turns writing down the
answers that the team agrees
on.

Step 4

Sign the paper to show that
you agree with the team's
answers.

Each teammate should sign the paper.

Wrap-up

Agree on answers to each of these questions.

1. What problem does the television-watching
   system solve?

2. What is your evidence that the parts of the
   television-watching system are interacting?

3. What are the parts of the television-
   watching system?

4. What is one variable in the system you could change to make C.Q. exercise **more** and still watch television? Draw a picture to show what this changed system would look like.

5. Suppose you made the change you suggested for question 4. What evidence would you look for so you would know that the variable had an effect on the system?

6. What is one variable in the system you could change so that C.Q. could exercise **less** and still watch television? Draw a picture to show what this changed system would look like.

7. Suppose you made the change you suggested for question 6. What evidence would you look for so you would know that the variable had an effect on the system?

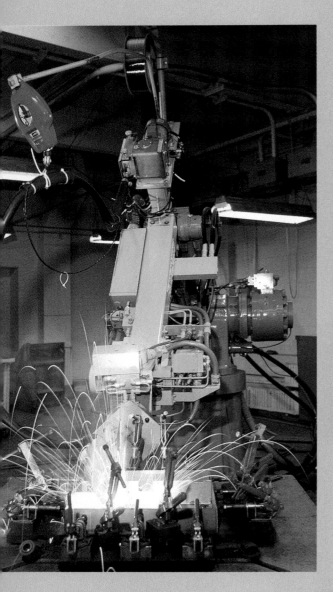
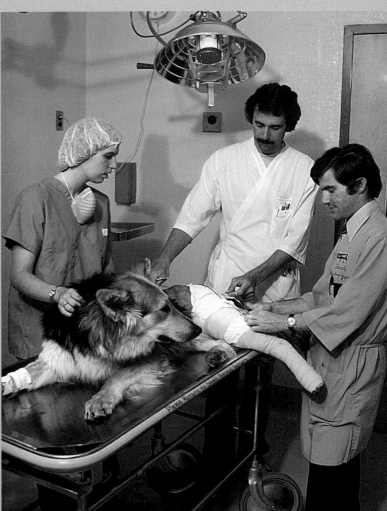

UNIT 3

Problems and Solutions

SYSTEMS AND ANALYSIS IN TECHNOLOGY

Introduction

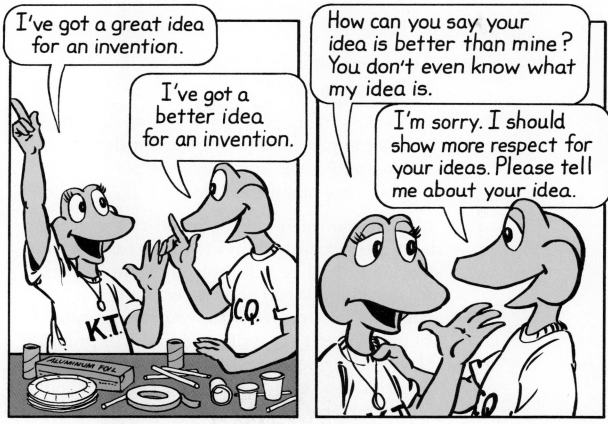

K.T. and C.Q. need to practice a new team skill: **Show respect for one another's ideas**. In this unit, you and your teammates will practice this new team skill, too. As a team, you will try to invent some systems for solving problems. The more ideas the team comes up with, the better the team's chances for solving the problems. Using the new team skill will help you and your teammates listen to more ideas and understand one another's ideas before you choose an idea to try.

You can practice this new skill by doing the following things:

- Ask someone else to tell you about an idea.

- Look at the person who is talking about the idea.

- Listen to the person talk about the idea. Don't interrupt.

- Discuss the idea with the person. You might ask the person a question about the idea. You might also encourage the person to tell you more about the idea.

When you listen to people and talk with them about their ideas, it shows that you respect their ideas. In turn, they will probably show respect for your ideas. When you respect your team-mates and they respect you, you will probably feel better about yourself. And you will probably enjoy working with your teammates more. Practicing this new team skill should help you and your teammates learn to get along better as you work on projects.

A Communication Problem

How do you get messages to others? You probably use many ways to communicate. You talk to others, you use a telephone, you send notes. Although you probably take these ways for granted, someone had to figure out how to do each of them.

"Nice Notes"

Here is a communication problem. The class must deliver a written message from everyone in the class to every other person in the class. You will use "nice notes" as the messages. When you say something nice to someone, that person usually feels better. Using "nice notes" gives you a chance to say something nice to your classmates.

Supplies

1 set of "nice notes"

1 list of the names of your classmates

scissors

pencil

On Your Own

Step 1

Look over all of the "nice notes."

Step 2

Decide who in your class should get each note.

It's easy to think of nice things to say about C.Q. I am having trouble with X.Z., but here's a good note!

Step 3

Write the name of each of your classmates on a "nice note."

Check off each classmate's name as you make a note. Make one note for each person in the class.

Step 4

Cut the notes apart on the dotted lines.

Step 5

When your teacher tells you to, deliver the notes to the right classmates.

Communicating by Mail

One way you can communicate with others is by writing letters and mailing them. Somehow the letter gets to the other person. As a project, you might want to find out how mail gets from the mailbox to the right person.

The story below describes what happened to some mail during the frontier days in the United States. As you read the story, think about these questions:

- What was supposed to happen to the mail?

- What was the plan to make it happen?

- Was the plan a system? (Think about the definition of a system.)

- Do people still use this plan? Why?

The Pony Express

(Adapted from The Pony Express: Hoofbeats in the Wilderness *by Joseph J. Dicerto)*

In the United States in the early 1800s, many things were changing. People were moving west. Cities were getting bigger. Industries were expanding. Transportation and communication were developing at high speed. Political views were becoming more extreme.

In the year of the Pony Express (1860), the United States was in a great crisis. News-making events, regarding the civil war to come, occurred rapidly. Communication between the East and Midwest worked well. Stagecoach lines, steam-engine trains, and even a telegraph line brought a daily flood of news as far west as St. Joseph, Missouri. However, news going farther west became an infrequent trickle. People in California and Oregon needed more immediate news of what was happening in the rest of the country. The nation needed a mail system faster than the several months it took ships to sail around the Cape or for wagon trains to move overland. That necessity gave birth to the idea of the Pony Express.

The plan was to establish a route that basically followed the old Oregon Trail. The route would start at St. Joseph, Missouri, pass through Kansas, Nebraska, Colorado, Wyoming, Utah, Nevada, and end in San Francisco, California, a distance of 1,840 miles (2,960 km).

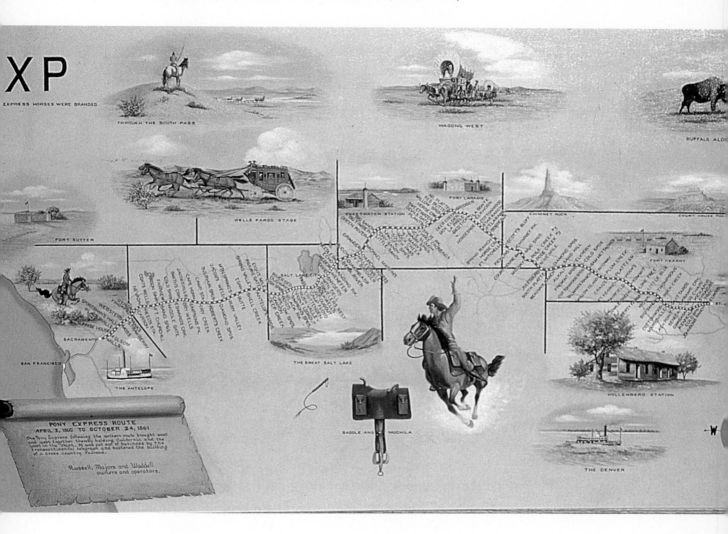

The service guaranteed delivery of mail (no packages) from St. Joseph to San Francisco in ten days. In order to accomplish this, the riders would have to drive their horses at top speed, with a change of animals occurring every 10 to 20 (16–32 km) miles. These locations were called relay stations. They were mostly rough, simple cabins, with a few stalls and a corral to maintain change horses. They were staffed by a stationkeeper and one or two helpers.

Pony Express riders rarely spent more than two minutes at the relay stations. They would leap off their horses, throw the mochila (a leather saddle bag that held the mail) over the saddle of the fresh horse, leap into the saddle, and wave good-bye. Stationmasters took care of the horses and had to be sure that change horses were saddled and ready for incoming riders.

There were also home stations along the route. Like relay stations, home stations had horse stalls, a corral, and fresh horses waiting to carry the mail farther along the route. However, when a rider arrived at a home station, he removed the mochila from his horse and threw it over the saddle of a fresh horse. Then a new rider would leap into the saddle and be off.

The Pony Express had 190 relay and home stations stretching across eight states, 420 horses, 400 stationmasters and helpers, and 80 riders. All of this had to be in place before the first rider could start. On April 3, 1860, the first rider left St. Joseph, Missouri at 7:15 P.M., just after a train arrived from the East bringing mail for the West Coast.

The astounding distance of the Pony Express's route was itself enough to challenge the endurance of the sturdiest team of riders. But distance was only part of the challenge. Along the way, Pony Express riders found nearly every type of natural surrounding imaginable, from roaring rivers to bone-dry deserts. They experienced equally varied weather conditions, from winter blizzards to the scorching heat of the desert. The winter of 1860-1861 was one of deep snows and unbearable storms. Many horses were injured because of the terribly hard riding conditions.

In 1860, both an Indian war and a civil war were brewing. The Indian war was a serious stumbling block, challenging the success of the service. When the fires of war flared, many of the stations were burned to the ground, stationmasters were killed, and equipment and horses were stolen.

From the moment of its birth in April of 1860, the days of the Pony Express were numbered. Nearly three decades earlier, a professor of art at New York University invented an electric signaling system. In 1843, Samuel Morse was given money to build a telegraph line between Washington, D.C., and Baltimore, Maryland.

THE TELEGRAPH.

A TERMINAL STATION.

The completion of a national telegraph line on October 26, 1861, was only one of many events that shortened the life of the Pony Express. Just before the start of the service, the company that established the Pony Express lost a great deal of money. Replacing the stations, equipment, and horses lost to the Indian wars would cost the company $75,000.

During its eighteen months of service, the Pony Express provided a dedicated and valuable service to the people of the United States. It had made a total of 308 complete runs, covering a distance of about 616,000 miles (995,000 km). The riders delivered 34,753 letters over mountains and deserts, through snow and rain storms, during the day and at night, across raging rivers, and past tribes of warring Indians. Only one mochila was lost.

Find the questions at the beginning of the story on page 160. Write answers to those questions.

A Better Way

Just like the people who planned the pony express, you had a problem—to deliver notes. You found a way to do that. You did get the job done. As with the pony express, your way worked, but you could probably find other ways to do the job. Your new problem is to deliver notes quickly and quietly.

TEAM TASK

Invent a plan for quickly and quietly delivering notes from everyone in the class to everyone in the class.

Team Skill

Show respect for one another's ideas.

Team Jobs

Communicator   Manager   Tracker

Team Supplies

1 set of "nice notes" for each teammate

1 list of the names of your classmates

paper and pencils

job clips for 1 communicator, 1 manager, and 1 tracker

Directions for a Better Way

Step 1

Brainstorm ways to send "nice notes" to your classmates more quickly and quietly than the class did the first time.

How to Brainstorm

- State any ideas that come to your mind.

- Record everyone's ideas. Do not judge whether the ideas are good or not.

- Keep thinking of ideas for at least five minutes.

- If you cannot think of an idea, add to or change an idea already on the list.

Step 2

Look at the list you brain-stormed. Choose one way that you think you would like to try, and plan how to make it work.

This is your team's plan.

Step 3

Be ready to explain your team's plan to the class.

The class will choose a few plans to try.

Step 4

Make a new set of "nice notes" to use when the class tests some plans.

Write classmates' names on a new set of "nice notes." Again, each teammate makes one note for each classmate.

Wrap-up

Talk about these questions with your team-mates. When you agree on an answer, each team-mate should write the team's answer. You will need the answers in a later lesson.

1. What did you want to happen to the notes using a system you invented?

2. How did you try to make it happen? (What plan did you use?)

3. What did you learn when you used the plan?

4. Would you use this plan again? Would you recommend this plan to others to use?

5. What can one person do to show respect for someone else's ideas? Think about what you or your teammates said that showed respect for another's ideas.

Stars of the Week

For the rest of the year, people in your class will be stars for one week. For each person who is a star, everyone in the class will write a "nice note." Your teacher will post the notes on a star somewhere in the room. Here are some ideas for messages you could write.

You are a good athlete.

You are kind to everyone.

I trust you.

You have great hair.

You are a loyal sports fan.

You always look good.

You are a good friend.

I wish I had your brain.

I like being around you.

You explain things so easily.

You have nice eyes.

You are a good leader.

You are fun to play with.

You treat people fairly.

I wish I had your manners.

You have great coordination.

You always seem happy.

You are a good sport.

You have a great smile.

You say interesting things.

You are very talented.

You always know what's going on.

You are easy to work with.

You have a nice voice.

You are a good observer.

I like how you think.

You are a good problem-solver.

You are a good listener.

You are really strong.

I like your sense of humor.

LESSON 14 Hovercraft

Do you notice anything unusual about the vehicle below? Does it have wheels? How do you think it moves?

The vehicle in the picture is a Hovercraft. A Hovercraft floats (hovers) on a cushion of air. It does not use wheels and does not need roads. It can travel over water as well as over land.

Hovercraft Uses

In 1953, Sir Christopher Cockerell built the first working model of a Hovercraft. Hovercraft work because air trapped inside the skirt fills the skirt and pushes against the skirt's sides. The air pushes up on the craft's bottom and lifts the Hovercraft. Then, the craft hovers.

Since Sir Cockerell's first invention, people have developed Hovercraft for many jobs. A Hovercraft ferry takes cars and people across the English Channel.

Some Hovercraft move heavy loads over rough, soggy, or icy areas. Some oil companies use Hovercraft to get to oil rigs in frozen or swampy places.

People also use Hovercraft in places where they do not want to damage the environment by building roads. Such places include the Florida Everglades and Brazil's upper Amazon River. A company in Sweden makes a lawn mower that uses an air cushion. It has no wheels that push grass down.

Hovercraft also provide entertainment. Skyleidoscope®, an air and water show at Disney World's EPCOT Center in Florida, uses ten hovering dragons. People who enjoy Hovercraft have even formed clubs. The Hoverclub of America holds rallies and races.

Making a Hovercraft

You and your teammates can build a Hovercraft. It won't be large enough for you to ride in, but you can make a model that will move like a large Hovercraft.

TEAM TASK

Build one craft that will move on a cushion of air.

Team Skill

Show respect for one another's ideas.

Team Jobs

Communicator

Manager

Tracker

Team Supplies

1 paper plate

1 toilet-paper tube

1 paper bag

1 metric ruler

masking tape

pencil

scissors

job clips for 1 communicator, 1 manager,
    and 1 tracker

Directions for Making a Hovercraft

Step 1

Cut the paper tube into three
shorter tubes.

Step 2

Stand a cut paper tube in the center of the paper plate and trace around the tube.

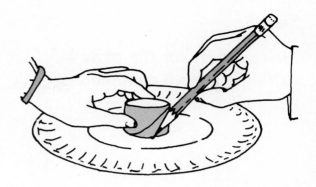

Step 3

Carefully cut out the circle you traced.

Divide the steps so everyone on the team helps.

Step 4

Gently push one end of the tube through the front of the plate.

The tube should fit snugly.

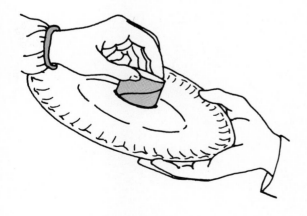

Step 5

Make a skirt for the plate by cutting a strip 5 centimeters wide from the paper bag.

The skirt should be a little longer than the tube.

Step 6

Tape the tube in place, and tape the skirt around the sides of the plate.

Be sure you completely seal the tube and the edge of the skirt.

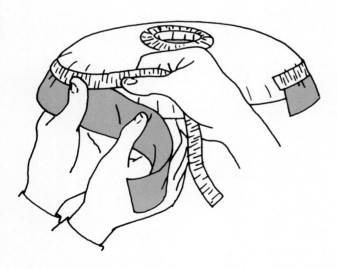

Step 7

Put the plate on a smooth, flat table or an uncarpeted floor. Make sure the tube does not touch the table or floor.

Step 8

Take turns blowing two or three times into the tube, and see what happens.

Step 9

Identify your Hovercraft in some way. Then, store it as directed.

Improving Your Hovercraft

At the end of this lesson, your team will move its Hovercraft through an obstacle course. To be ready for that challenge, test your Hovercraft to see how well it moves over or around obstacles. Invent ways that you think will make the Hovercraft move better.

TEAM TASK

Decide on one or two ways to change the team's Hovercraft so it will move through an obstacle course more easily. Make the changes and test the Hovercraft again.

Team Skill

Show respect for one another's ideas.

Team Jobs

 Communicator
 Manager
 Tracker

Team Supplies

the team's Hovercraft

pencil and paper

supplies the team selects

job clips for 1 communicator, 1 manager, and 1 tracker

Directions for Improving Your Hovercraft

Step 1

Set up some obstacles to test whether your team can make its Hovercraft move over or around the obstacles.

Step 2

Decide on at least one change the team wants to make in its Hovercraft.

You may build a new Hovercraft or make changes in the one you already built.

We could use a longer tube and make it stick up to catch the air. We could use a different shape for the craft, use a different material for the skirt, make the skirt a different size, use a blow dryer and try hot air. . .

Step 3

Make the changes.

Step 4

Test the changed Hovercraft.

Step 5

Decide whether the Hovercraft does what you want. If it doesn't, make more changes and repeat Steps 2 through 5.

Step 6

Answer the Wrap-up questions. Be ready to explain your team's answers to the class.

Wrap-up

Decide on answers to these questions with your teammates. Write the team's answers on your own paper. Save the papers to use later.

1. What was the problem you wanted to solve with your Hovercraft?

2. How did you try to solve the problem?

3. What did you learn when you tried your new craft?

4. What did you do next?

5. What is one example of how you or a teammate showed respect for someone's ideas?

Invent a System

Thingamajig

by Alan J. McCormack

What on earth is a thingamajig?
Small and blue? Red and big?
Can you use it on Mondays to brush your teeth?
Is it made of cardboard with springs underneath?

Did you see someone use one while painting a wall?
Was it made from balloons and a squashed rubber ball?
A thingamajig could be heavy or light,
Something to use to make the world bright.

A tiny contraption to catch a gray mouse,
Or an elephant scrubber as big as a house.
Make it from any old junk that you find;
A thingamajig grows in your mind!

In 1913, Alfred Clark invented this thing-amajig. Can you guess what problem Mr. Clark wanted to solve?

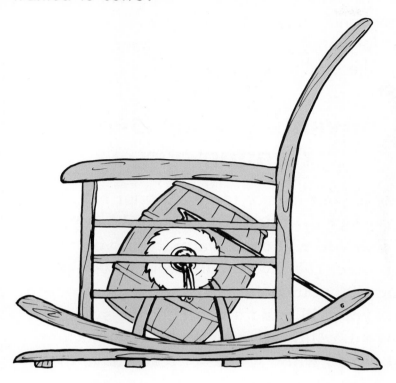

Mr. Clark invented his thingamajig because he had a problem. He liked butter on his toast in the morning, but in those days, people couldn't buy butter at the store. They had to make their own butter in a hand-operated butter churn. Mr. Clark thought that churning butter by hand was very hard work. He wanted an easier way to make the butter.

To solve his problem, Mr. Clark invented a thingamajig—a new system for churning butter. His new system worked by combining the two tasks of churning butter and rocking in a chair. He named his thingamajig "Alfred Clark's Rocking-Chair Butter Churn."

Mr. Clark's new churn helped him make butter as he rocked in his chair. All he had to do was pour cream into the barrel that was attached to the chair and rock away the hours. If he rocked for enough hours, the thingamajig would change the cream into butter.

Inventing Your Own Thingamajig

Now is your chance to invent your own thingamajig—your own new system to solve a problem. First, you will choose a problem you would like to solve. Then, you will invent a system, a thingamajig, you could use to solve the problem. Finally, you will build a model of the system you invent. (Although your model should look as if it would work, it doesn't really have to work.) When you finish, be ready to show others your thingamajig and tell what it does.

You will work alone to complete this task. If you need help coming up with ideas or building your model, ask your teacher or another student for help.

Supplies

any supplies you choose from the "junk" table

paper and pencil

On Your Own

Step 1

Think of a problem you would like to solve.

Ask yourself, "What problem do I have that a new system could solve?" If you need help, check with another student or with your teacher.

My books are too heavy to carry to school every day. I'd like to invent a system that would carry my books for me.

Step 2

Think of a thingamajig you could use to solve the problem.

Ask yourself, "What will this new system look like? How will it work?"

Step 3

Build a model of a thingamajig you could use to solve the problem.

Use any supplies you want from the "junk" table to build your model. Your model doesn't really have to work, but you should be able to use the model to explain to others how your new system would work.

Step 4

When you finish building your model, answer these two questions on your own paper.

- What was the problem you wanted to solve?
- What system did you invent to solve the problem?

Step 5

Be ready to show the model to your classmates, and tell them about the problem you tried to solve.

Solving Problems by Answering Questions

Do you remember reading about Alfred Clark's rocking-chair butter churn? You might wonder why you have never seen one of those thingamajigs. If it was such a great system for making butter, why don't people still use Mr. Clark's thingamajig? The answer is that Mr. Clark's system wasn't easy enough. Mr. Clark set out to solve the problem of finding an easier way to churn butter. His rocking-chair butter churn made butter, but it took too long. Alfred Clark decided that it was just as hard to use his rocking-chair butter churn as it was to churn butter by hand. Mr. Clark decided that he needed a different system to solve his problem.

If you think about it, you realize that Mr. Clark asked and answered four questions as he solved the problem of making an easy-to-use butter churn. Here are the four questions that helped him solve the problem.

1. What do I want to happen?
(What problem do I want to solve?)

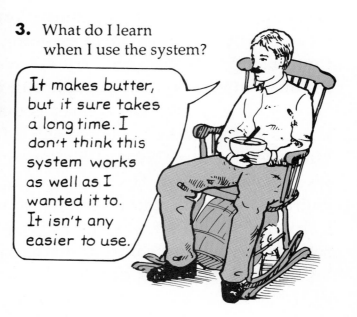

> I want to make a new system for churning butter – one that is easier to use than this hand-operated butter churn.

2. How can I try to make it happen?
(What system could I invent to solve the problem?)

> I'll build this rocking-chair thingamajig. It should be a lot easier to use.

3. What do I learn when I use the system?

> It makes butter, but it sure takes a long time. I don't think this system works as well as I wanted it to. It isn't any easier to use.

4. What could I do next?

I know what to do! I'll build a different system. If I attach an electric motor to the butter churn, I won't have to work to churn the butter. A different system could solve my problem.

Comparing Answers

Do the four questions seem familiar to you? They should. You and your teammates answered the same questions in Lesson 13, "A Communication Problem," and Lesson 14, "Hovercraft."

Four Questions to Ask and Answer While Solving a Problem
1. What do you want to happen? (What is the problem you want to solve?)
2. How can you try to make it happen? (What system could you invent to solve the problem?)
3. What do you learn when you use the system?
4. What could you do next?

TEAM TASK

Compare the team's answers to the Wrap-up questions from Lessons 13 and 14 with another team's answers. Find out how each team's answers are alike and how they are different.

Team Jobs

Communicator   Tracker   Checker

Team Skill

Show respect for one another's ideas.

Team Supplies

the team's answers to the Wrap-up questions from Lessons 13 and 14

job clips for 1 communicator, 1 tracker, and 1 checker

Directions for Comparing Answers

Step 1

Compare the team's answers to the Wrap-up questions from Lesson 13 with the team's answers to the questions from Lesson 14.

Decide how the team's answers are alike and how the team's answers are different for each lesson.

Step 2

Compare your team's answers from Lessons 13 and 14 with those of one other team.

Decide whether the other team gave the same answers that your team gave. Also decide whether the other team came up with the same solutions that your team did.

Step 3

CHECKER: Check that the team completed the team task.

If the team is finished, let your teacher know. If not, keep working until the team is finished.

Discussion Questions

Discuss these questions with your classmates.

1. Look at the four questions to ask and answer while solving a problem. Did you ask and answer all four of the questions when you made a model of your thing-amajig? Why or why not?

Four Questions to Ask and Answer While Solving a Problem

1. What is the problem you want to solve?

2. What system could you invent to solve the problem?

3. What do you learn when you use the system?

4. What could you do next?

---

2. If you made a thingamajig that really worked instead of just a model, would you ask and answer all four of the questions? Why or why not?

How old do you have to be to invent a system to solve a real problem? Would you believe that you are old enough already? If you don't believe that, read the following news report about a real invention. As you read, think about the four questions to ask and answer while solving a problem. Casey Golden asked and answered the four questions as he solved his problem. Try to figure out how Casey answered each of the questions.

Boy promoting biodegradable tee

Evergreen 12-year old shows product in Japan

by Steve Caulk
Rocky Mountain News Staff Writer

A world-class product deserves worldwide exposure.

With that in mind, 12-year-old Casey Golden of Evergreen [Colorado] traveled to Japan recently, where he introduced the item he says will make him a millionaire: a biodegradable golf tee he invented.

Environmentally conscious golfers will love it, he says.

Better yet, greenskeepers could insist on it, says Casey's father, John Golden.

Made of recycled materials and water-soluble binders, the tees are coated with a substance that deteriorates in sunlight. Judges in a national competition for young inventors selected Casey's tee as the most impressive entry in his age category a year ago.

"Something that irritated me was, when I was golfing, my dad always told me to pick up the broken tees," he said. "I didn't understand why. I couldn't use them anymore. Well, he was a greenskeeper's helper in high school, and he said the greenskeepers got annoyed when they mowed the tee boxes and had to pick up the broken tees."

For one thing, the tees don't look good. For another, the tees occasionally bounce into the mower's blade, dulling it and sometimes jamming it.

Casey's award-winning tee was originally made of grass seed, fertilizer, applesauce, and peat moss. But when his father began investigating the marketing potential, he discovered that greenskeepers couldn't accept the grass seed and fertilizer tees because their ingredients might not blend with the grass on the course.

Otherwise, the greenskeepers have been enthusiastic, John Golden said.

"I attended the golf course superintendents conference in Orlando [Florida]," he said. "They control what goes on their golf courses. And they told me I couldn't make enough of them."

A policy restricting tees to the biodegradable variety would send golfers scurrying to Golden's product.

So far, the Goldens have produced only a couple hundred tees, using them to attract potential distributors.

"We'll charge a premium," said John Golden. "But we can compete with the wooden tees."

He has filed a trademark affidavit, and he says he plans to file a foreign patent with Akira Aoki of Japan, the man who sponsored Casey's recent trip.

John Golden believes the biodegradable tee will become particularly popular in Japan, where wood is at a premium and golf is one of the few excuses the Japanese use to take off from work.

In the United States, 2 billion golf tees are purchased each year, he said. That equals 40,000 birch trees.

Casey's first priority in life, he says, is to do well in school. After that, he wants to become rich.

When he does, he plans to enlarge his bedroom and install a skylight, he says.

Next on his list of things to invent: a golf ball that never litters the rough.

Wrap-up

Discuss these questions with your classmates.

1. What problem did Casey Golden want to solve?

2. What system did Casey invent first to solve the problem?

3. What did Casey learn when he tried his first system?

4. What did Casey do next?

Foam Follies

Some inventions do not work the way you want them to. When that happens, you might think that you failed. Below is a true story about an invention that failed. But this failure ended up making millions of dollars. Read "The Failure That Made Millions." As you read, think about **what the inventors did next**, after they tested the invention.

The Failure That Made Millions

Spencer Silver's job was to invent a new kind of glue. The 3M company wanted him to invent a glue that was stronger than any other glue on the market.

Mr. Silver could not solve the problem the 3M Company wanted him to solve. He thought that his invention might have a use. Because he could not figure out a use, he showed it to others and asked for their help. When no one had any ideas, Mr. Silver gave up and worked on solving other problems.

Arthur Fry, another chemist at 3M, knew about Mr. Silver's invention. One day, Mr. Fry thought of a use for the removable glue.

Although Mr. Silver failed to solve the problem he wanted to solve, he solved a different problem. Mr. Fry helped find a use for the removable glue. The glue was not perfect at first, but Mr. Fry did not give up. He kept making changes until he found something that solved the new problem.

Today, the 3M Company sells pads of note paper that use removable glue. They call the pads Post-it Notes. Lots of people use sticky notes every day. Have you ever used a sticky note?

Discussion Questions

1. Did Spencer Silver fail? Explain your answer.

2. What problem did Spencer Silver want to solve?

3. What problem did Spencer Silver and Arthur Fry actually solve?

4. What did Spencer Silver do when his invention did not solve his problem?

Here's a Solution: What Is the Problem?

Spencer Silver solved a problem with his removable glue. It was not the problem he tried to solve at first, however. Sometimes, as Spencer Silver did, people invent something and find a use for it later.

Now, you and your teammates will do what Spencer Silver and Arthur Fry did. You will take C.Q. and K.T.'s invention and find a use for it. Then, you will decide how to advertise it so people will want to buy the foam and use it for the purpose your team chose.

TEAM TASK

Find a use for the foam C.Q. and K.T. invented. Make an advertisement that would make someone want to buy the foam.

Team Jobs

Communicator

Manager

Checker

Team Skill

Show respect for one another's ideas.

Team Supplies

25 milliliters of a gelatin mixture

1 teaspoon of baking soda

1 teaspoon of alum

1 empty cup

1 tray

1 stirrer

1 pair of goggles for each teammate

1 sheet of construction paper, 12 by 18 inches

nontoxic markers

paper towels

paper and pencils

job clips for 1 communicator, 1 manager, and 1 checker

Directions for Here's a Solution: What Is the Problem?

Step 1

Decide which teammate will be in charge of the baking soda, who will add the alum, and who will pour the gelatin mixture.

Step 2

Put on your goggles.

Step 3

Make the foam by combining the following in the large cup in this order:
• baking soda
• alum
• gelatin mixture

You might want to mix the foam, using a stirrer.

Step 4

Observe the foam and notice its properties.

 Do not taste the foam. Wipe up spills right away.

Step 5

Brainstorm a list of possible uses for the foam.

Step 6

Decide on one use for the foam that solves a problem.

Step 7

Write and draw an advertisement that would make people want to buy the foam for the use the team chose in Step 6.

What will the ad tell people about the problem? What will the ad say about the foam itself?

Step 8

Be ready to present your team's ad to the class.

You could show your ad. You could also act out someone using the foam.

Wrap-up

Present your ad to the class. See how many of your classmates would buy the foam if it were for sale.

LESSON 17

Bookrack Challenge

By now, you should be getting good at solving problems. Here is a chance to solve another problem. As you work on it, think about whether your system is the only solution to the problem. Think about how you solve problems.

Making a Bookrack

Have you ever wanted something that would hold a book for you? It would allow you to read yet have your hands free. Your team's problem is to make such a bookrack. The only materials you may use are newspapers and masking tape. The bookrack must hold the book at an angle so you can read it. It must also lift the book at least four centimeters off the table.

TEAM TASK

Using only newspaper and tape, make a bookrack that will hold a paperback book at an angle so you can read it. It must also lift the whole book at least four centimeters off the table.

Team Skill

Show respect for one another's ideas.

Team Jobs

Communicator

Manager

Checker

Team Supplies

1 ruler

1 paperback book

newspaper

masking tape

job clips for 1 communicator, 1 manager, and 1 checker

Directions for Making a Bookrack

Step 1

Be sure everyone understands what problem you are trying to solve.

Step 2

Talk about several different systems you could invent to solve the problem.

Step 3

Decide on one system you will try.

Step 4

Build the system using newspapers and tape.

Remember that all teammates should help.

Step 5

Test the system by putting a book on it.

Did the system solve the problem?

212

Step 6

Decide what you will do next,
and do it.

Could you make the bookrack better
by changing anything? Should you
start over and invent a different system? Are you satisfied with your system and ready to stop?

Be ready to discuss these questions with the
class.

1. How many times did you test bookracks
   before you felt that your system solved the
   problem?

2. How did the problem-solving questions
   help you solve the problem?

3. Is there more than one system that could
   solve the problem?

4. How could you and your teammates improve at using the team skill: **Show respect
   for one another's ideas**?

Systems for Solving Problems

> *Some people see things as they are and ask why.*
> *I dream of things that never were and ask why not.*
>
> **—Traditional Motto of Inventors**

In this unit, you learned that people can solve problems by inventing systems. Each system is something new, whether it is a new way of doing something or a new tool or machine (a thingamajig). Sometimes, the systems work well. Other times, the systems need improvements.

In this unit, you also learned that people usually ask and answer the following four questions as they solve a problem.

Four Questions to Ask and Answer While Solving a Problem

1. What is the problem you want to solve?

2. What system could you invent to solve the problem?

3. What do you learn when you use the system?

4. What could you do next?

Solving a Drinking Problem

This lesson will help you show how much you have learned about inventing systems for solving problems. There are two parts to this lesson. You will work with your teammates to complete each part.

TEAM TASK

Read about a real system that Marvin Stone invented to solve a drinking problem. Decide how Marvin Stone would answer each of the four questions to ask and answer while solving a problem.

Team Jobs

Communicator

Tracker

Checker

Team Skill

Show respect for one another's ideas.

Team Supplies

paper and pencils

job clips for 1 communicator, 1 tracker, and
1 checker

Directions for Solving a Drinking Problem

Step 1

Read "A System That Lets You Drink Without Touching the Glass" on pages 218–220.

Step 2

As a team, decide how Marvin Stone would answer each of the following questions.

1. What problem did Marvin Stone want to solve?
2. What system did he invent to solve the problem?
3. What did he learn when he first used the system?
4. What did he do next?

Step 3

Write down the answers.

Step 4

Sign the paper to show that
you each agree with the
answers.

Step 5

Give the paper to your teacher.

A System That Lets You Drink Without Touching the Glass

In 1888, Marvin Stone invented a system for
drinking without touching the glass. He invented
the first paper drinking straw. In those days,
people didn't have air conditioning. To cool off
on hot summer days, people drank cold drinks,
such as lemonade. Sometimes, the people would
sip their cold drinks through natural straws cut
from the stalks of wild grasses. Marvin Stone
didn't like sipping his lemonade through a straw
made of grass. He thought the natural straw
made the drink taste funny.

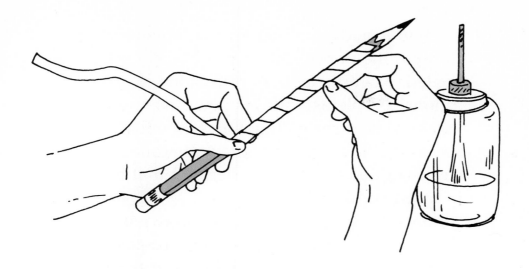

To solve that problem, Marvin Stone wrapped a long thin strip of paper around a pencil and glued the loose end to keep it from unwinding. Then, he slipped the paper tube off his pencil and into his lemonade. When people saw the artificial straw that Marvin had invented, they wanted one, too.

People enjoyed sipping their lemonade through the paper straws that Marvin Stone invented. Nevertheless, Marvin Stone saw two additional problems with his new invention. First, lemon seeds kept getting stuck in the straws. Second, if he drank the lemonade too slowly, the straws got soggy. Marvin decided that he needed to improve his straws.

Marvin Stone improved the straws by making the tube too narrow for the seeds to pass through and by coating the paper with wax. Mr. Stone's drinking straws became very popular. Since that time, many other people have improved on Mr. Stone's invention. Perhaps you have seen some of these other types of systems that let you sip lemonade without touching the glass.

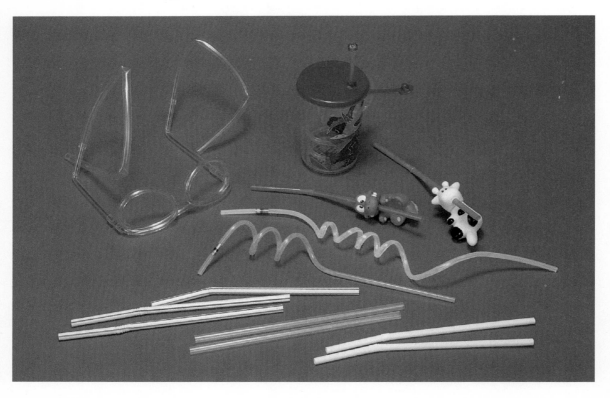

Solving a Sticky Problem

C.Q. and K.T. wanted to solve a sticky problem, but instead they got stuck! Now, they think they have failed. Read about the problem that C.Q. and K.T. tried to solve. Decide what they could do next.

TEAM TASK

Decide what C.Q. and K.T. could do next about a sticky problem they wanted to solve.

Team Jobs

Communicator

Tracker

Checker

Team Skill

Show respect for one another's ideas.

```
┌─────────────────────────────────────────────────┐
│  Team Supplies                                  │
│                                                 │
│  paper and pencils                              │
│                                                 │
│  job clips for 1 communicator, 1 tracker, and   │
│      1 checker                                  │
│                                                 │
└─────────────────────────────────────────────────┘
```

Directions for Solving a Sticky Problem

Step 1

Read "A System for Making Homemade Glue" on page 224.

Step 2

As a team, decide how C.Q. and K.T. might answer each of the following questions.
1. What problem did C.Q. and K.T. want to solve?
2. What system did they invent to solve the problem?

3. What did they learn when
   they used the system?
4. What are two different things
   they could do next?

Step 3

Write down the team's
answers.

Step 4

Agree on an answer to this
question: "Did C.Q. and K.T.
fail?"

Write down the team's answer.

Step 5

Sign the paper to show that
you each agree with all of the
team's answers.

Step 6

Give the paper to your teacher.

A System for Making Homemade Glue

Wrap-up

Answer these questions on your own paper. Be ready to share your answers with your classmates.

1. What are two different ways that you can show respect for someone else's idea, even if you disagree with the person's idea?

2. Why is it important to show respect for other people's ideas?

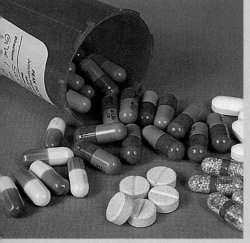

UNIT
4

Self and Substances
SYSTEMS AND ANALYSIS IN HEALTH

Introduction

C.Q. and K.T. are working on a project together. Each of them has a job to do. K.T. is trying to take over C.Q.'s job, as well as do her own. How do you think that makes C.Q. feel?

As you work in this unit, you will practice a new team skill: **Avoid put-downs**. Put-downs can be direct. When K.T. said, "You don't cut as neatly as I do," she was putting C.Q. down. She was saying that she was better than he was. When people call someone else names, that is a put-down.

Put-downs can also be indirect. Taking over for someone else and finishing someone else's sentence are examples of other put-downs. Those actions show that one person thinks he or she can do something better than another person can.

In the cartoon above, K.T. offered to help C.Q. She did not say he could not do the job. She did not say he was doing a bad job. She let C.Q. decide whether he needed or wanted help. K.T. avoided putting C.Q. down.

When you work with others, you will sometimes disagree. You will also have different ways you work. Avoiding put-downs does not mean that you always agree. It does mean that when you disagree you tell your idea. You do not call someone else's idea stupid. You share ideas. You think about which idea is best for that task. Other ideas are often good ideas for the task or for some other task.

Think of some put-downs you have seen or heard. What did the person say? What did the person do? What could the person have said or done instead?

Think about how people feel when someone puts them down. How do you think C.Q. felt in the first scene? How do you think he felt in the second scene? How could avoiding put-downs help teams work better?

LESSON 19 Drugs, Drugs, Everywhere

What is a drug? Do drugs affect you, your family, your school, and your community?

I don't understand how drugs can affect so many people.

C.Q.

You

Your School

DRUGS

Your Family

Your Community

In this unit, you will analyze how drugs affect you and others.

What Do You Know About Drugs?

You have probably heard a lot about drugs, and you already have some ideas about drugs. To find out what you already know, answer the following questions. You will not show this paper to anyone else, unless you want to.

Questions About Drugs

Write the numbers 1 through 10 on a piece of notebook paper. Next to each number, write your answer to a question. Use "Yes," "No," or "?" Write "?" if you are not sure of the answer.

1. Have you ever seen drugs used on television?
2. Have you ever seen drugs advertised on television?
3. Are drugs ever harmful?
4. Are drugs ever helpful?
5. Is it legal to use drugs?
6. Can you always predict how drugs will affect you?
7. Do people ever invent new drugs?
8. Do you think most people use drugs?
9. Have you ever been bothered because someone else used drugs?
10. Have you ever used a drug?

Getting the Picture

Because this unit is about drugs, your class needs to agree on what a drug is. You and your teammates will find pictures of drugs and make a collage. As you make your collage, you will have to decide what is and what is not a drug.

TEAM TASK

Make a team collage, showing many kinds of drugs. Then, write a team definition of the word "drug."

Team Skill

Avoid put-downs.

Team Jobs

Communicator

Manager

Tracker

Team Supplies

1 sheet of construction paper

magazines

unlined paper

scissors

nontoxic markers

nontoxic glue

container for scrap paper

paper and pencils

job clips for 1 communicator, 1 manager, and 1 tracker

Directions for Getting the Picture

Step 1

Each teammate, cut out five pictures you think show drugs.

Step 2

Show your teammates your pictures.

Step 3

Talk about whether you think each picture is a drug and why.

Does everyone agree? If someone disagrees, that person should explain why. If the team agrees that a picture does not show a drug, the person who found that picture should find another picture.

Step 4

To make a team collage, arrange all the pictures on one sheet of construction paper. Glue the pictures in place.

Step 5

Sign the collage to show you agree that all the pictures are pictures of drugs.

Step 6

Throw away or recycle scrap paper and clean your work area.

Step 7

MANAGER: Return the supplies.

Step 8

COMMUNICATOR: Put the collage on a bulletin board.

Step 9

Discuss what the word "drug" means. Then, decide on a team definition for the word "drug."

Step 10

Write on a sheet of paper the team's answer to "A drug is something that _____ ."

The definition should fit all the pictures on the team's collage. Be sure everyone on your team agrees with and can explain the definition.

Wrap-up

You have heard your classmates' ideas about drugs. Look at your answers to the Questions About Drugs on page 234. Have your ideas about what a drug is changed? If so, make any changes you want in your answers.

Homework

Drugs usually affect the people who use them. Sometimes, drugs affect people who don't use them. Write a short paragraph about someone who had a problem because another person used drugs. You might know someone with such a problem. You might have read about someone with a problem. You might have seen on TV someone with a problem. Do not use real names in your story.

LESSON 20 Under the Influence

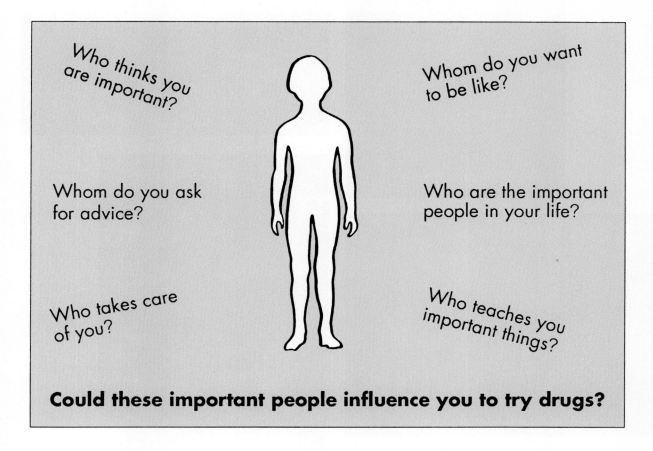

Who thinks you are important?

Whom do you want to be like?

Whom do you ask for advice?

Who are the important people in your life?

Who takes care of you?

Who teaches you important things?

Could these important people influence you to try drugs?

You and the people who influence you form systems. As you know by now, a system is a group of objects that interact. The parts of a system can be people as well as objects. When people influence you, they have interacted with you. You have formed systems with them.

Who Influences You?

When all the parts of a system are people, a system is called a **social system**. Everyone is part of many social systems. You are part of a school system, a family system, and several systems of friends.

Your class at school is a system. The parts include you, your classmates, and your teacher. You interact with your teacher. You ask and answer questions, turn in written work, and follow class rules. You interact with your classmates. You work in a team, you talk, and you pass papers to one another.

Analyzing Your Family System

You belong to a family system. The parts might be a father, a mother, a stepparent, sisters and brothers, stepsisters, stepbrothers, and you. Each family system is different. You might have many brothers and sisters, or you might have none. You might have one parent or two. Your grandparent or a cousin might be part of your family system. A pet might be important to you and be part of your family.

There are different ways to define families. How would you define your family system? Would you include only the people you live with? Would you include others who are important to you? Is everyone who lives with you part of your family? To understand your family better and to answer questions, such as those above, analyze your family system.

On Your Own

Step 1

Identify the parts of your family system.

Who are the people in your family? Who interacts with you? Write their names.

Step 2

Draw lines between people's names to show who influences each person.

Are some interactions stronger or more important? Make those lines darker or thicker.

Step 3

On each interaction line, write a word or two describing some evidence of the interaction between the two people.

How do they influence each other? How do they communicate?

Predicting What Will Happen If . . . ? in Family Systems

In Unit 2, you analyzed the respiratory system. Then, you predicted how the system might change if you added cigarette smoke. In this lesson, you analyzed the family system. One reason for analyzing systems is to solve problems, such as how to make accurate predictions.

Here is a problem for you to solve: Predict what would happen in your family system if you smoked. Before you make your prediction, you should make some observations. One way of observing is to ask questions. Ask family members questions to find out their feelings about smoking.

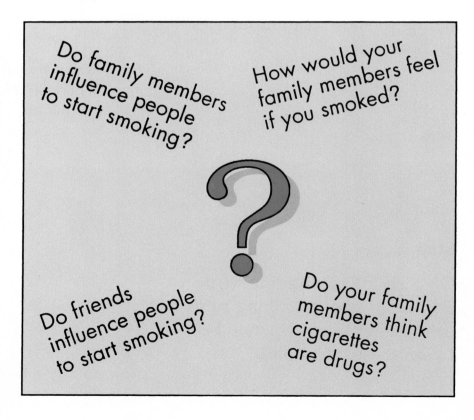

Do family members influence people to start smoking?

How would your family members feel if you smoked?

Do friends influence people to start smoking?

Do your family members think cigarettes are drugs?

On Your Own

Step 1

Ask a family member to
answer your questions.

You may interview another adult if
no one in your family can help you.

Step 2

Ask the questions on the interview sheet, The Smoking Habit.

Step 3

Write the answers on the interview sheet.

You may use the back or extra
paper, if you need more space to
write on.

Step 4

Thank the person.

Discussion Questions

You interviewed someone in your family
about smoking. Discuss with your class what
you found out.

1. Did anyone influence your family
   member's decision about smoking?

2. Does your family member like to be around smoke?

3. Would your family member approve if you smoked?

4. Does your family member think cigarettes are drugs? Why?

How would **you** answer the following interview questions?

5. Do you like to be around smoke?

6. Would you approve if a friend smoked?

7. Do you think cigarettes are drugs? Why?

Other Social Systems

What other social systems are you in? Are you in scouts? Are you on a sports team? Do you go to a church or synagogue? Those are all social systems.

Everyone in the class is part of at least two social systems besides the family. You go to school. You are part of a classroom system. You have friends. You are part of one or more systems of friends. You might belong to several different systems of friends.

Each person's social systems are different. So, you must identify the systems yourself.

On Your Own

Step 1

Trace the figure below onto the center of a piece of paper. The figure is supposed to be you.

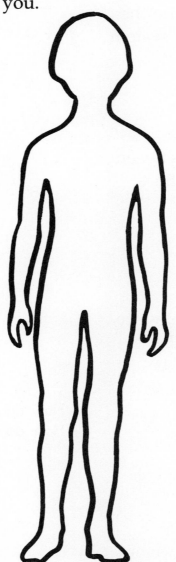

Step 2

Identify a system (group) you are part of. Write a name for the group at the top of the paper.

Step 3

Around your figure, write the names of people in that system who influence you.

Step 4

Show the interactions between the people by drawing lines connecting the names.

Step 5

On each interaction line, write a few words that describe evidence of interactions between the two people.

How do the people communicate? How do they influence each other?

Wrap-up

Write your answers to the following questions on a paper. Give the teacher your paper when you are done.

1. Who are three people who influence you in some way?

2. What do you predict would happen in your family if family members found out that you smoked or used another drug?

3. Think of another social system you are part of. What do you predict would happen in that system if members found out that you smoked or used another drug?

Homework

During the rest of the unit, look for stories about people who use drugs. Bring the stories to school. Share them with your classmates. You may also write your own story to share.

Smoke Gets in Your Lungs

You learned about the breathing system in the science unit. Can you answer these questions?

- What is the purpose of the respiratory system?

- What are the parts of the system?

- What changes did you predict would take place if someone added cigarette smoke to the system?

We studied that a long time ago! Now, I need to test my memory.

If you cannot answer the questions, review "A Breathing System," starting on page 127.

The Cleanup Crew

Look at this picture of the respiratory system.

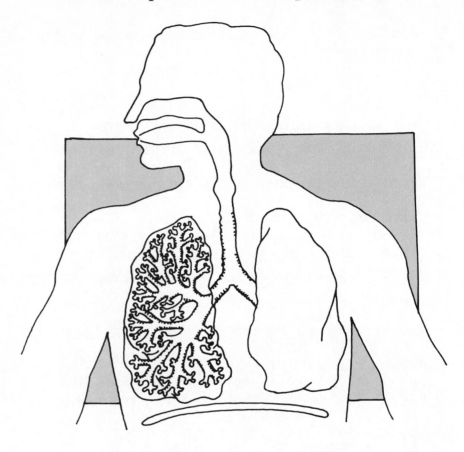

Tiny hairs, called **cilia**, cover most of the system. The cilia are part of the body's cleanup crew. They move back and forth like a wave and sweep out dust and dirt.

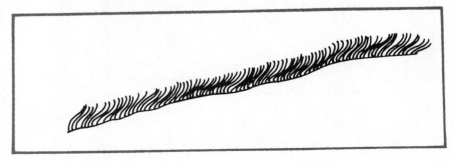

When a person smokes, thick, dark tar coats the cilia.

As a class, you saw how a sticky substance, molasses, coated a jar. Tar sticks to cilia in much the same way. Imagine how hard it would be to walk through mud up to your waist. That is how hard it is for cilia to move when tar coats them.

Paralyzing the Cleaners

Cigarette smoke has many chemicals in it. Some, like those in tar, coat the cilia and make it hard for the cilia to move. Other chemicals paralyze the cilia for a short time. Paralyzed cilia cannot move.

Each time a person smokes, the cilia stop working for a while. Tar gets into the lungs and coats the cilia. When the cilia can again move, they move slowly because of the tar. If they have a chance, the cilia will get the tar out after a while. But, if the person smokes another cigarette, the cilia stop and more tar builds up.

Think about what you know about the respiratory system. What do you think would happen to a person's lungs if the person smoked every day for many years?

That looks like a question we ask when we do analysis.

Cigarettes and Health

Early in the 1900s, people did not know that smoking was harmful. Some doctors predicted that it might be harmful, but they could not prove it. In 1958, Dr. E. Cuyler Hammond and Dr. Daniel Horn described a test they did. They tested cigarettes as a variable for causing deaths. Read the story and look for answers to these questions.

- What questions did Dr. Hammond and Dr. Horn ask about cigarettes and health?

- What are some variables they looked at?

- How did Dr. Hammond and Dr. Horn test the variable?

- Did they use a fair test?

This story, from *Highlights for Children*, explains what Dr. Hammond and Dr. Horn did.

Disease Detectives:

Scientists Who Solve the Mysteries of Illness

by Elizabeth Feuer

How would you like to solve a crime and catch a killer red-handed—without using a gun to do it? Some of the world's most dangerous killers have been tracked down and caught by scientists armed with nothing more than pencil and paper.

These scientists are the detectives of the medical world. Most are specially trained doctors. They study all kinds of things that affect our health, everything from diseases to food poisoning to car accidents. Officially they are called **epidemiologists** (eh puh DEE mee OL uh jists). Let's just call them disease detectives. . . .

Of all the great work of the disease detectives, I think the greatest was giving us the proof that cigarettes are bad for our health. You've heard many times that smoking can cause cancer, bronchitis, and heart attacks. More than thirty years ago many doctors *thought* that was true but had no evidence. Naturally the makers of cigarettes wanted—and still want—people to smoke. They said there was no real evidence that smoking made people sick. Some nonsmokers also get lung cancer, and many smokers live to a ripe old age. So, how can you prove that cigarettes are bad?

There were other difficulties. A person infected with [a cold] gets the disease quickly. But it may take years to see the effects of smoking. And more than one factor may contribute to some diseases. Air pollution and other factors may contribute to lung cancer.

Here was a real challenge to the disease detectives. Their hunt for the killer was the greatest in history. They kept health records on many thousands of men, smokers and nonsmokers, from cities and farms and from different parts of the country.

For all those who died, medical records were tracked down to find the cause of death. Of those who died from lung cancer, 397 were regular cigarette smokers. Only 15 had never smoked. To see the effect of smoking, we need to compare the same *numbers* of men, and men of the same age. When we make that comparison, we get the results [on the next page]. You can see that cigarette smokers die from lung cancer more than 10 times as often as nonsmokers. . . .

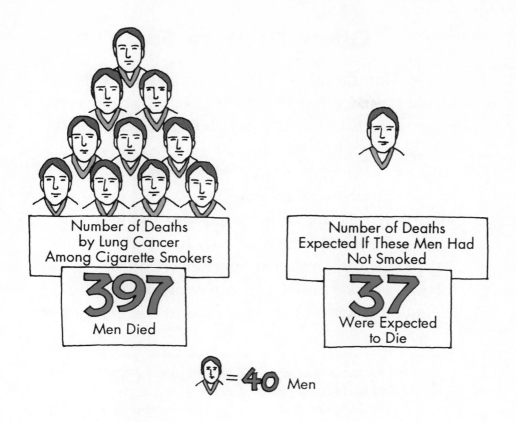

Number of Deaths
by Lung Cancer
Among Cigarette Smokers

397

Men Died

Number of Deaths
Expected If These Men Had
Not Smoked

37

Were Expected
to Die

= **40** Men

Drs. E. Cuyler Hammond and Daniel Horn were the master detectives who showed that cigarettes are killers. They kept records for 44 months on 187,783 men of ages 50 to 69. About 100,000 were regular cigarette smokers, about 50,000 smoked some, and about 30,000 never smoked. . . .

Lung cancer was only one of many causes of death that were studied. Not all diseases were affected by smoking, but the surprise was the large number of different diseases affected by smoking. All combined, the chance of death was 64 percent higher among cigarette smokers than among nonsmokers.

Now you know why all packages of cigarettes have a label warning that cigarettes may injure your health. Cigarettes are killers because they increase the risk of lung cancer and other diseases. That's what the disease detectives proved.

Other Tobacco Facts

Dr. Hammond and Dr. Horn observed that smokers had more heart attacks and strokes than nonsmokers. Other disease detectives observed that children of smokers have more colds than children of nonsmokers.

What questions do you have about those observations? Think about what you know about colds and about tars and cilia. Read the following paragraphs about two other chemicals in tobacco smoke. See if you can answer the questions you asked at the beginning of this paragraph.

Tobacco smoke contains nicotine and carbon monoxide. Nicotine makes the heart beat faster than normal. The heart needs energy from oxygen to beat. When people smoke, they breathe carbon monoxide instead of some of the oxygen. Their hearts work more but have less oxygen. In addition, people get addicted to nicotine. Once they get used to using it, they do not feel good if they stop.

Some doctors studied people who are around cigarette smoke but who are not smokers. They found that people around cigarette smoke had tar in their lungs. Those people also had nicotine and carbon monoxide in their bodies.

Wrap-up

Write one of the letters described below. Give evidence to explain what you write.

1. Pretend you are a respiratory system. Think of messages about smoking that you would like to give to the person you are inside of. Write a letter to that person.

2. Write a letter to a person you know who smokes. Tell the person how you feel about smoking and why. Tell the person how you feel when you are around someone who is smoking and why.

LESSON 22

Instead of Drugs

Money to Burn

C.Q. thought K.T. was crazy when she asked if he would burn a dollar. Yet, smokers burn money every time they light up. With your team, figure how much money a smoker burns in one year.

TEAM TASK

Figure how much money a smoker spends on cigarettes in one year.

Team Skill

Avoid put-downs.

Team Jobs

Checker   Communicator   Tracker

Team Supplies

1 calculator

paper and pencil for each teammate

job clips for 1 communicator, 1 checker, and 1 tracker

Directions for Money to Burn

Step 1

Decide how many packs of cigarettes a day a smoker might smoke.

Step 2

Figure how many packs that person smokes in a week and then in a year.

Years have 52 weeks.

Step 3

Find out how much one pack of cigarettes costs.

Step 4

Figure how much a smoker spends on cigarettes in one day, one week, and one year.

Everyone should help decide how to solve the problem. You may use a calculator.

HINT: You know how many packs the smoker smokes in a day, a week, and a year. You know how much one pack costs. What can you do with these numbers to figure out the cost of cigarettes?

Step 5

Everyone, record the team's answer.

Wish List

If you had the money a smoker spends on cigarettes, how would you use it? You figured how much money it costs to smoke for one day, one week, and one year. Now, decide how you would use that cigarette money.

TEAM TASK

Assume you had the money a smoker spends on cigarettes in one week or one year. Make one list showing how the team would use the money.

Team Skill

Avoid put-downs.

Team Jobs

Manager   Tracker   Communicator

Team Supplies

1 calculator

catalogues and brochures

paper and pencil for each teammate

job clips for 1 communicator, 1 manager, and 1 tracker

Directions for a Wish List

Step 1

Each teammate, list several ways you would like to use the money that a smoker spends on cigarettes in one year.

Step 2

Use "Choices" on page 270 and the catalogues and brochures to find out how much money each item on your list would cost. Write the cost next to the item.

Step 3

Teammates, take turns reading items from your lists.

On your first turn, read what you would like to do most.

Step 4

Choose some uses for the money that everyone on the team wants.

Choose at least one item from each teammate's list.

Step 5

When you agree on a way to spend the money, everyone should write that choice down and record its cost.

Step 6

Subtract that amount from the amount of money left.

Use the calculator, if you have one.

268

Step 7

Repeat Steps 3 through 6 until
the money is gone.

Step 8

Decide on team answers to the
Discussion Questions.

Be ready to explain your team's
answers to the class.

Discussion Questions

1. What would happen to family members if
   someone in a family started using drugs,
   such as cigarettes?

2. If someone in a family stopped using
   drugs, how do you think a family might
   use the extra money?

Write your own answer to this question:
Would you rather spend money on drugs or
on other things? Why?

Choices

Listed below are some items students in other classes chose to "spend their cigarette money" on. The prices below show what things cost in their towns when students "spent" the money. The prices might be different for you.

meal at a fast-food place	$ 4.00
comic book	.75
movie	4.00
video rental	3.00
1 hour of horseback riding	15.00
1 ticket for a professional sporting event	10.00
skateboard	50.00
bicycle	100.00
trip to visit a relative in a nearby city	100.00
coat	75.00
sneakers	30.00
one week at camp	250.00
music lessons—1 week	10.00
music lessons—1 year	400.00
10 karate/judo lessons	80.00
1 video game	70.00
computer	1,000.00
television	300.00
portable radio/tape player	100.00
personal tape player	25.00
music on cassette tape	8.00
bus pass for 1 month	10.00
bike lock	4.00
aquarium setup	30.00
telephone	30.00
skates	25.00
donation to help others	_____
deposit in savings account	_____

LESSON 23 Saying No to Drugs

The pressure's on
So maybe you will
Smoke or drink
Or take a pill.
It can be at home
Or on the street
From a stranger
Or a friend you
   meet.
You may deny it
But we say it's so.
Do you know how
To just say No?

271

Resisting the Pressure

If someone tried to influence you to smoke, drink, or use another drug, could you resist the pressure? Just saying no does not always work.

Here are steps to take if someone pressures you to do something you don't want to do.

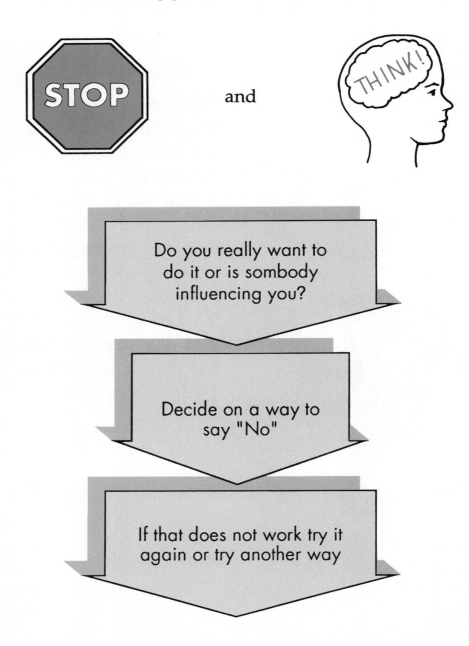

STOP and THINK!

Do you really want to do it or is sombody influencing you?

Decide on a way to say "No"

If that does not work try it again or try another way

Ways to Say No

If you do not want to do something, say no. There are many ways to say no. All problems do not have the same solutions. Practice the following ways to say no. Be ready to use them when you need to.

Be assertive. Tell the person how you feel, but do not make the other person angry.

Change the subject. Suggest doing something else.

Say something funny. Turn the offer into a joke.

Question your friendship. Ask if the person likes the real you or the you who will use drugs.

Stall. Delay making any decision about what you will do.

I don't feel like it right now.

I don't need it yet.

Shift the blame. Explain that someone else will not let you do it.

My parents won't let me.

No one in my family does it.

Ignore the offer. Pretend you did not hear the offer.

Just turn your head and talk to someone else.

Just walk away

Practice, Practice, Practice

To be able to say no when you want to, it helps to practice. At first you might feel strange using some of the ways to say no. With practice, you will feel more natural. Then, you will be ready to say no when you want to.

TEAM TASK

Do a skit that shows one way to say no to a drug-related problem.

Team Skill

Avoid put-downs.

Team Jobs

Communicator

Manager

Checker

Team Supplies

3 Problem Cards

1 Solution Card

job clips for 1 communicator, 1 manager, and 1 checker

Directions for Practice, Practice, Practice

Step 1

Each teammate, take one Problem Card.

Step 2

Each teammate, decide how to use the solution on the team's Solution Card for your situation.

Step 3

Explain your problem and your solution to your teammates.

Step 4

As a team, choose one of the
problems and plan a skit. In
the skit, use the team's solution
for saying no.

Each teammate must be in the skit.

Step 5

Act out the skit.

Step 6

The class will guess which solution your team used.

Wrap-up

Think about the solutions for refusing to use
drugs. Decide which ways are best for you.
Write two ways you might really use.

Hold the Medicine

Do you use over-the-counter drugs? You probably have seen many of them at home and on commercials. These drugs have many uses.

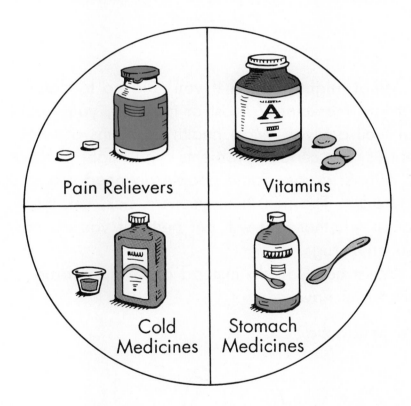

Pain Relievers

Vitamins

Cold Medicines

Stomach Medicines

Some people use a lot of over-the-counter drugs. Often, they do not think that taking a drug has any risk. They could say, "Hold the medicine. I'll try something else first." Is that another way to say no?

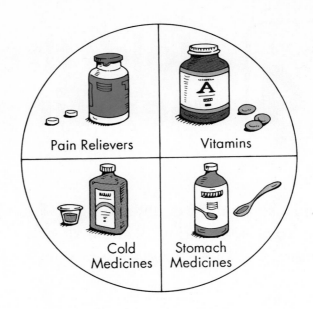

What might happen if you said no to drugs that are medicines? Most of the time, you would get well anyway. Most health problems are not serious. For serious problems, you might get sicker without drugs. Some people do need drugs to stay alive. The next time you are sick, ask the doctor whether you will get better if you do not use any drugs.

What can you do instead of taking a drug when you have

• a headache?

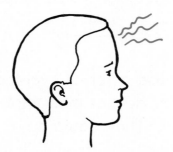

- an upset stomach?

- a sore throat?

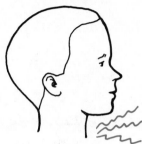

- sore muscles?

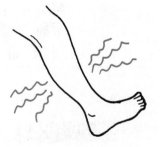

- trouble staying awake?

- trouble sleeping?

What's the Choice?

If you decide not to take the medicine, you might want to do something else to feel better. People have used many remedies to feel better. With your teammates, you will choose some remedies you think might help with each problem. You could suggest other remedies also.

TEAM TASK

Match each problem with a remedy that is not a drug.

Team Skill

Avoid put-downs.

Team Jobs

Communicator

Checker

Tracker

Directions for Choosing Remedies

Step 1

Divide these problems so each
teammate has two to deal with.
- headache
- upset stomach
- sore throat
- sore muscles
- trouble staying awake
- trouble sleeping

Step 2

Each teammate, write your two
problems on a sheet of paper.

Step 3

Each teammate, choose **remedies** from the list that you think might help the problems you selected.

Each problem has several remedies. Some remedies help more than one problem.

Remedies

  a. Gargle with warm, salt water.
  b. Listen to quiet music.
  c. Soak in warm water.
  d. Relax your whole body.
  e. Exercise your neck and shoulder muscles.
  f. Get some fresh air.
  g. Get extra sleep.
  h. Use a heating pad.
  i. Melt a hard candy in your mouth.
  j. Drink plenty of liquids.
  k. Read a book.
  l. Drink a "flat" soft drink.
  m. Exercise hard.

Step 4

Each teammate, write the remedies you chose next to the problems you chose.

Step 5

Show your teammates your answers and talk about them.

Step 6

Be ready to explain your answers and your teammates' answers to the class.

To Use or Not to Use

Sometimes, people use drugs when they do not need to. There are times when people should use drugs. For example, some diseases happen when a person's body does not work right. A person with diabetes does not have enough insulin to use the sugar that the person eats. Most people's bodies make insulin. A diabetic often needs the drug insulin or another drug that helps the body make insulin. Without the drug, the diabetic would get sick and could die.

It is also a good idea to use a drug in other situations. For example, a person should take a drug for a strep throat. A germ called streptococcus bacteria causes strep throat. If the germ stays in the body, it can move to the heart and cause a more serious illness called rheumatic heart disease. Drugs called antibiotics, such as penicillin, kill the bacteria. Then, the person not only gets better but also does not get a more serious illness.

Some kinds of drugs protect people from getting sick. Before you started school, you got immunizations. These drugs keep you from getting diseases that used to harm, kill, or cripple a lot of children. Most young children get immunizations to protect them from tetanus, whooping cough, diphtheria, polio, measles, mumps, and German measles.

Wrap-up

With your teammates, make a list of questions or clues you could use to help you decide whether to use a drug.

Can You Handle It?

You have analyzed social systems and found some ways that people interact. One type of interaction is to influence others. Influence can affect the choices you make. It can help you make good choices, but it can also lead you to make poor choices. Within some social systems, members influence one another to use drugs. In other social systems, members influence one another to stay away from illegal and harmful drugs. The final choice, however, is always yours.

Another way that members of social systems interact is by helping one another. From time to time, everyone has problems that are too big for one person to handle alone. The people you could ask for help make up your **support system**.

The use of drugs can create problems that people need help for. Sometimes, people cannot stop taking a drug even when they want to. Those people are addicted to the drug, and they need help. Sometimes, families suffer because a family member uses drugs. Then, the family might need help. When drug dealers control a community, the community needs help.

Identifying Your Support System

Your support system includes people whom you can ask for help. A person in that system might help you solve your problems. That person could help you get more help. Sometimes, the support person helps by listening and letting you know someone cares about you.

Do you know where you could go for help if you had a problem? What if someone in your family had a problem? What if a friend had a problem? Are there people in the social systems you analyzed who could be part of your support system?

Step 1

Look at the analyses you did of your family and of another social system.

Step 2

Choose one or two people from each system you could talk to if you had a problem.

Step 3

Write down their names.   This is your support system.

The Drug Scene

Your team will put on a two-act skit that shows a drug problem. At the end of your skit, do not show that everything is okay. Every situation is different. You probably cannot predict a real-life ending. The skit should show that you know how to say no and how to ask for help.

TEAM TASK

Plan a two-act skit about a drug problem.

Team Skill

Avoid put-downs.

Team Jobs

Teammate 1—A drug user (friend)

Teammate 2—The decision-maker (you)

Teammate 3—A support person

Team Supplies

You will not need supplies for this task.

Directions for the Drug Scene

Step 1

Read the situations below.
Choose one.

a. A friend shows you a can of beer in a school desk.

b. A friend smokes marijuana behind the school building and offers you some.

c. A friend accidentally drops some crack from a book and offers you some.

d. Your next-door neighbor offers you a beer.

e. Your friends offer you some chewing tobacco.

f. A friend is smoking marijuana in the park and offers you some.

g. A friend asks you to hold some cocaine for someone else.

h. A friend offers you some alcohol on the school bus.

i. A friend shows you some drugs hidden at home and offers you some.

Step 2

Decide who will play each part.

The parts are listed under Team Jobs. You could pick numbers on pieces of paper, or you could choose the part you want.

Step 3

Read about the drug for your team's situation.

Information about the drugs starts on page 296.

Step 4

Decide who your support person is.

Is the support person a teacher, friend, parent, coach, scout leader, or someone else?

Step 5

Work on Act 1 using the following plan.

- Teammate 3 will explain the situation.
- Teammate 1 will offer teammate 2 a drug.
- Teammate 2 will refuse the offer.

Use at least one piece of information you read about the drug in Step 3, and use a strategy to say no.

- Teammate 1 will say, "I really don't want to use drugs either, but I can't stop."

Step 6

Work on Act 2.
- Either teammate 1 or 2 will explain the problem to teammate 3.
- Teammate 3 will ask some questions and then say, "Here's what you might do."
- End the play.

Do not tell what to do.

Step 7

Practice your play. Present it to the class.

Wrap-up

Look at the analysis of your family again. Predict what would happen to your family system if you added a drug.

1. Pick a drug. Do not pick cigarettes. Pick one of the drugs described on the following pages or another drug you have heard about. It should be a drug that is illegal for children to use.

2. Decide who in the family will use (interact with) the drug.

3. Predict how the family system might change.

What About Alcohol?

Alcohol is a colorless liquid. It is found in beer, liquor, and wine. It slows the body down and changes the drinker's mood.

People act different when they drink alcohol. Some people get sleepy. Others get mean. Some people get quiet. Others get loud. Drinkers do not think clearly. Sometimes, a drinker passes out. Alcohol mixed with other drugs can cause death.

Many adults can drink a little alcohol with no problem. But people who drink a lot of alcohol can damage their brain, heart, liver, and pancreas. If a pregnant woman drinks, alcohol can harm her baby.

Alcohol can also damage families. Sometimes, people who drink too much alcohol feel alone and guilty. They might have problems with their jobs or with money. They often cause car accidents that hurt others.

People can get addicted to alcohol. Treatment involves several steps. The addicted drinker must admit there is a problem with alcohol, stop drinking, and allow his or her body to get rid of the alcohol. The addicted drinker must learn not to drink. One support system for addicted drinkers who do not want to drink is Alcoholics Anonymous.

Family members often have problems, too. They need help. Groups like Alateen and Al-Anon can serve as support systems for the families of people who are addicted to alcohol.

What About Marijuana?

Marijuana comes from the dried leaves, flowers, seeds, and stems of the cannabis or hemp plant.

People act different when they smoke marijuana. Some marijuana users feel happy, sleepy, or confused. Some users have problems breathing. Some cannot move smoothly. Sometimes, a user has trouble remembering.

People who use marijuana for a long time can develop lung diseases. One marijuana cigarette adds more tar to the respiratory system than one tobacco cigarette does. People who smoke marijuana for a long time have more infections than those who do not smoke marijuana. People between the ages of 11 and 15 who use a lot of marijuana sometimes do not grow normally.

Some marijuana smokers have trouble quitting. They might need help to stop smoking marijuana.

What About Cocaine or Crack?

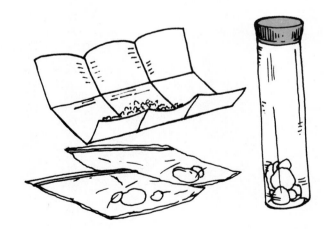

Cocaine is a white powder made from the leaves of the coca bush. Crack is a stronger and more deadly form of cocaine. It often looks like small stones.

Cocaine speeds up the workings of the brain and the nervous system. People sometimes talk a lot when they use cocaine. For a short time, they have a lot of energy and feel very self-confident. Later, users become depressed and cranky.

People who use a lot of cocaine can destroy the inside of their nose. Some users become very afraid of everything and have trouble sleeping. Cocaine can cause convulsions and death.

Crack makes people feel more energetic than cocaine does. It works faster but lasts a shorter time. People can become addicted to crack after using it only one time. Some researchers say that death is possible (from seizures, stroke, or heart attack) every time a person uses crack.

Cocaine and crack cost a lot more money than cigarettes. People who are addicted often spend hundreds of dollars a day on these drugs. They often sell drugs or steal things to get money for drugs.

Some cocaine users and many crack users have trouble quitting when they want. They often need help to stop using these drugs.

What About Smokeless Tobacco?

Chewing tobacco and snuff—smokeless tobacco—are made from tobacco leaves. Chewing tobacco is a wad of tobacco leaves. Snuff is tobacco ground into small pieces.

Smokeless tobacco affects the body in several ways. All tobacco contains the drug nicotine. Nicotine first speeds up and then slows down the workings of the brain and heart. Smokeless tobacco causes bad breath and stained teeth. People who use smokeless tobacco are less able to taste and smell than those who don't use it. People who use smokeless tobacco have more tooth decay and gum disease than normal.

People who use smokeless tobacco often get white patches inside their mouth. Sometimes, these white patches turn into cancer of the mouth and throat. Just like cigarettes, smokeless tobacco can cause cancer, heart disease, or stroke.

People can become addicted to all forms of tobacco. There are support groups for people who want to stop using tobacco.

Deciding About Drugs

The time has come,
For you to decide.
When the choice is yours,
Where will you side?

On Your Own

Step 1

Your teacher will assign you a situation from "The Comic Strips" that follow. You decide

- Who might influence you if you were in the situation?

- Who might care about your decision?

- What would your body decide?

- What would you decide if you were in the situation?

Choose a real person in your life, not a person in the comic.

Choose real people in your social systems.

Explain what the drug might do to your body.

Explain why.

Step 2

Then, use one refusal strategy from Lesson 23 and say no to drugs.

The Comic Strips

1.

Sally really likes the rock group the Granite Pebbles.

The Granite Pebbles are famous and use drugs.

Sally thinks she might use cocaine to be like her idols.

2. Steve wants to be part of a certain group at school.

Members of the group talk about the stuff they use in their special place.

Steve knows that to join the group he will have to smoke some marijuana.

3.

James wants to look good.

Many good looking people he sees in magazine ads are smokers.

James feels that he should smoke cigarettes to look good.

4. Patti is tired of looking like a baby. She wants to look older.

Patti sees some of the older students smoke.

Patti thinks that she'll look older if she smokes cigarettes.

5.

Glenda wants to change her image. She thinks she is boring. In the movies, most of the exciting people drink alcohol.

Glenda thinks that using alcohol would add excitement to her life.

6.

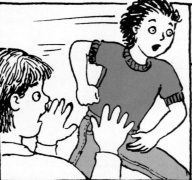

Bobby's friends say he's hyper. His friends yell at him for being too excited.

He has read that some drugs slow a person down.

Bobby wonders if smoking marijuana will help him calm down.

7.

He has heard that some drugs make you feel happy. Scott thinks that crack might make him feel happy.

Scott feels rotten. He doesn't even know why.

8. Carole is angry with her parents.

She knows that they would be upset if she used drugs.

Carole thinks she might try marijuana just to make her parents angry.

9. David's friends often tease him.

Most of them chew tobacco. David thinks he might give in to the peer pressure and try some chew.

10. Susanne feels alone. She wants to be like everyone else.

The drug users at school always seem to have friends.

Susanne thinks that using crack might bring her new friends.

Send a Message

You have influence
On others you know.
So share what you've learned
And help them to grow.

Think about what you have learned in this unit that you think others should know. Think about what messages you would like to share with others. You and your teammates will put your message on buttons or a poster. When you finish, you will put your work where others can see it.

If you are going to make buttons, go to the section called "Making Buttons." If you are going to make a poster, follow these directions:

Making a Poster

TEAM TASK

Make one poster with a message about drug use.

Team Skill

Avoid put-downs.

Team Jobs

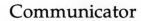

Communicator

Manager

Checker

Team Supplies

1 poster board

crayons or nontoxic markers

paper

job clips for 1 communicator, 1 manager, and 1 checker

Directions for Making a Poster

Step 1

As a team, decide on the message about drugs you want to tell others.

Step 2

Plan your poster.

Decide what pictures you want, where the pictures should go, and where the words should go.

Step 3

Make a sketch of the poster on notebook paper.

Step 4

Decide who will do each part of the poster.

For example, one person could do the pictures; another could do the words.

Step 5

Make sure the poster has everything the team decided on, and check the spelling.

Step 6

Sign the poster and hang it up.

Making Buttons

TEAM TASK

Your teacher will explain whether each person makes a button or whether the team makes one. If each person makes a button, everyone on the team should use the same message.

Team Skill

Avoid put-downs.

Team Jobs

Communicator

Manager

Checker

Team Supplies

drawing circle(s)

plastic button cover(s)

button back(s)

nontoxic markers

paper

job clips for 1 communicator, 1 manager, and 1 checker

Directions for Making Buttons

Step 1

As a team, decide on the message about drugs you want to tell others.

Step 2

Plan your button.

Decide what pictures you want, where the pictures should go, and where the words should go.

Step 3

Make a sketch of the button on notebook paper.

Step 4

Make the button circle and
decorate it.

When you write the message on the
circle, do not go all the way to the
edge of the paper.

Step 5

Follow the teacher's directions
and use the button maker.

Step 6

Be sure you know which button is yours.

Step 7

Hand in your button.

Wrap-up

Write your own answers to these questions.

1. What drugs do you think you will have a
   chance to use?

2. What decisions do you think you will
   make? Why?

3. Could your decisions hurt you?

4. Could they hurt others? If so, whom?

ACKNOWLEDGMENTS

Text

"The Case of the Invisible Radon" on pp. 57–58 is reprinted by permission of National Geographic Society from the September 1990 issue of *National Geographic World*, Washington, D.C.

"Lynx vs Game Boy," text and photos, on pp. 83–89, copyright 1990 by Consumer Union of United States, Inc., Mount Vernon, NY 10553. Reprinted by permission from *Zillions*, August/September 1990.

"The Respiratory System" on pp. 143–145. Special permission granted by *Current Health* Magazine, published by Field Publication. Copyright © 1990 by Field Publications. *Current Health* is a federally registered trademark of Field Publications.

"The Pony Express" on pp. 160–166 is adapted from the book *The Pony Express: Hoofbeats in the Wilderness* by Joseph J. DiCerto. Copyright © 1989 by Joseph J. DiCerto. Reprinted by permission of the publisher, Franklin Watts, Inc.

Activity on pp. 177–181 is adapted from "Hovercraft Test Pilots" in *WonderScience*, August 1987. Used by permission of the American Chemical Society, Washington, D.C.

"Boy Promoting Biodegradable Golf Tee" on pp. 197–199 is reprinted by permission from the *Rocky Mountain News*, Denver, CO.

"Disease Detectives" on pp. 257–259 is adapted by permission from *Highlights for Children, Inc.*, Columbus, OH. Copyright © 1990.

Photo

Photo research by Carlye Calvin, Nederland, Colorado.

All photos, including cover, by Carlye Calvin except as follows:

W. Perry Conway: cover photo (b)
Dave B. Fleetham/Tom Stack and Associates: cover photo (l)
The Granger Collection: p. 163, p. 164, p. 165
Lowell Observatory: p. 26 (t) (b)
D & I MacDonald/Unicorn Stock Photos: p. 244
Doug Martin: p. vi (t, r) (t, l), p. 1, p. 64 (b), p. 152 (l) (r) (b), p. 226 (t) (b), p. 227
Tom Myers: p. 175 (t)
NASA: p. vi (b)
Claude Pierrelouis: p. 173
Pony Express Museum: p. 161, p. 166
Karelle Scharff: p. 64 (l)
Werner Schultz: p. 114

World Wide Photo: p. 174, p. 175 (b)

Wyoming State Archives, Museums and Historical Department: p. 162

Key: (t) top, (b) bottom, (l) left, (r) right, (c) center

Art

Meg Kelleher Aubrey, Eulala Conner (Publishers' Graphics), Pamela Donahue, Ruth Flanigan, Sally Laffely, Diana Magnuson (Craven Design), Cheryl Kirk Noll, Roz Schanzer (Craven Design), Andrew Smith, Dave Sullivan

Editorial, design, and production services provided by **The Book Department, Inc.**